# PRAISE FOR
# ONCE UPON A ROAD TRIP

- "Once Upon A Road Trip reminds us how special it is to find love in a chaotic world."
    **-- The Kindle Book Review**

- "A powerful story of self-discovery."
    **-- IndieReader Review**

- "What a grand adventure! Angie deems her tale, 'running away from destiny, or headlong into it,' and takes the reader cross-country and into Canada on a charmingly wacky 6,000 mile jaunt."
    **-- Portland Book Review**

- "A true coming-of-age memoir, and a fabulous read."
    **-- InD'tale Magazine**

- "Blount's debut coming-of-age tale is charming. Readers ride shotgun, gazing at the beautiful landscapes and meeting the interesting people Angeli discovers while traveling from Minnesota to New York and beyond."
    **-- RT Book Reviews**

- "All 6,000 miles of Angie's road trip make for an exceptional, un-mediocre story."
  **-- San Francisco Book Review**

- "*Once Upon A Road Trip* is an engaging read with lots of interesting developments that keep the reader hinged to see what will happen next."
  **-- LITERARY CLASSICS**

- "A beautiful coming-of-age story that defines its genre and takes the reader on an odyssey they'll never forget! What a wonderful debut!"
  ***-- #1NYT bestselling author*** **Rachel Van Dyken**

# Once Upon An Ever After

Angela N. Blount

Published by Artifice Press®

ISBN: 978-0-9895809-6-0

Copyright © 2014 by Angela N. Blount
Cover photography by Danielle Barnum
Cover art by Revalis
Editing by Courtney Wichtendahl

An Artifice Press book / published by arrangement with the author

ONCE UPON AN EVER AFTER

Library of Congress Control Number: 2014914538

For more information, or to receive written permission, address: Artifice
Press
PO Box 22472
Huntsville, AL 35814
http://www.artificepress.com

Printed in the United States of America

## Disclaimer

This anthology is a continuation of the account in the memoir, *Once Upon A Road Trip*. Events and conversations have been depicted to the best of my recollection—several years after the fact, and with the assistance of actual journal entries/emails used for documentation. Some incidents and dialogue have been condensed for the ease of retelling. Names and identifying details have been changed or omitted to protect privacy. It is only my intention to tell my story, not to cause anyone harm or defamation.

~Angela N. Blount

*For my husband – for never giving up on our story.*

"Love is the strongest force the world possesses, and yet it is the greatness of a road leading toward the unknown."

— General Charles De Gaulle

# Preface

"So...I hear you picked up a souvenir boyfriend on that road trip of yours," Alan said, turning the conversation personal for the first time that evening.

Of course, we were at the end of our allotted hangout time—with me about to drop him off at his house. And of course, I was in a hurry to get back home. I'd known Alan most of my life, and he never did have a keen sense of timing. Still, I hadn't seen him since high school graduation, and a *lot* had happened in the last three months.

"That's one way of putting it," I shrugged, pulling my car to a stop under the circling light of the street lamp in front of his parent's modest, two-story home. It was a balmy early September night in Minnesota, and the crickets seemed to know they were running out of time before cold weather set in. Their desperate chorus of chirping drifted in through my open car windows. "I didn't really mean to, he just...refused to give up."

"The last time I refused to give up on a girl, I'm pretty sure it ended in a restraining order," Alan laughed, a tight raspy sound. I wasn't entirely sure he was joking. I'd known him since childhood, and his scrapes with the law bordered on legendary. "It's just kinda weird," he went on, voice carrying blatant intrigue. "You finally pick somebody, and he's on the opposite side of the country. That long distance thing has to be tough."

"Yeah," I said, grimacing. "But I figure if we can handle this, we can handle just about anything." I put my car in park and turned to look at him.

Ever the thrill-seeker, Alan hadn't bothered putting on his seatbelt. He held one arm draped along the passenger window while the rest of his compact form pivoted in my direction. Alan had tousled white-blond hair, eyes as blue as the sky on a subzero day, and the kind of Scandinavian-fair complexion that only came in two shades depending on sun exposure: pasty white, and lobster red. He liked to claim he was descended from some ancient Viking chieftain, but I was reasonably sure it was just an attempt to impress girls...and/or excuse his propensity for causing senseless property damage.

While I was off traipsing around half of North America by car over the summer, Alan was causing car-related problems for roughly half the population of our hometown. First he'd stolen a friend's Jeep and played pinball with it between a guard rail and a handful of other vehicles. Now on probation with his license revoked, he was under suspicion of using a high-powered BB-gun to take out the back windows of several hundred parked cars. He wasn't admitting anything one way or the other, and I wasn't sure I wanted to know.

"I never would have guessed you'd be the type," he went on, puzzling something out aloud.

"What type?" I asked, trying to hurry him to the point. He didn't seem to notice my impatience.

"To up and fall in love with some internet guy you just met." His sandpapery tone was taunting, intended to get a rise out of me.

It worked.

"First of all, Vince and I had been friends for a long time before I met him on the road trip," I corrected, flexing my hands around the steering wheel. "And I didn't 'fall in love'," I added, with a liberal use of air quotes. "I geared up, anchored a rope, and made a controlled descent into love."

*Okay, so that didn't sound particularly romantic.*

But oh, how I despised that saying. Sinkholes...abandoned wells...vats of industrial acid—those were the kinds of things people "fall into." They also "fall short," "fall ill," and "fall in line." For me there was no falling involved at all. I'd counted the cost and made a choice, simple as that.

"So, it's serious?" Alan asked, scrutinizing me with an intensity that unsettled my stomach. Or maybe it was the stale scent of cigarette smoke clinging to him that made me queasy—reminding me of someone who didn't deserve a place in my memory.

"You make it sound like a terminal ailment," I countered, chuckling to dispel my own discomfort. I caught myself doing an unconscious check for the can of Mace I kept alongside my emergency brake.

"Yeah, well...these things usually *are* terminal. One way or another." Cynicism added a trace of coolness to his demeanor. Alan was putting on his best 'bad-boy trying to be deep' impression, and I wasn't sure what to make of it. He had never pretended to care about my personal life before...so why now?

"You think I'd be putting myself through this if it wasn't serious?"

"Probably not." He smirked, regarding me with an almost calculating thoughtfulness. "You always were the most practical girl I knew."

"Gee, thanks." I rolled my eyes, hands still fiddling with the steering wheel in front of me. "As compliments go, that's right up there with 'dependable' and 'good team player.'"

I was wielding sarcasm like a shield, I realized. I shouldn't be so unnerved to be alone with a guy-friend in a car. It was just Alan. We'd grown up together — trading sibling-like insults and the contents of innumerable school lunches. But so much happened over the summer, my perceptions seemed forever altered.

Or maybe "damaged beyond repair" was more accurate. After all, it was the misjudging of one of my best guy-friends that had caused me so much lingering pain. So far the only person I'd trusted with my freshly wounded state was Vincent, the sweet-yet-troubled boy I'd tried to leave behind after visiting Alabama. The only one who really knew me.

Alan cracked an amused smile. "I'd ask if he's good to you, but I figure you'd have neutered him by now if he wasn't."

I laughed. Okay, so maybe Alan knew me a little.

"He's pretty great," I said, sobered by the reminder that I hadn't actually seen Vince in over four weeks. "But he's going to worry if I don't get back and make our nightly phone date." Vince had called earlier in the evening, while I was in the middle of watching a movie with Alan and my parents. I had promised to call him back once I'd ferried Alan back home, but Vince sounded dejected over the delay. I didn't want to make him wait any longer than I had to.

"Boyfriends before bros, huh?" Alan's white-ish brows raised in mock-offense. "I see how it is."

"Says the guy who can't seem to give *any* of his friends the time of day whenever he's got a new girlfriend," I shot back, making no effort to hide my irritation.

"Whoa, easy," Alan raised both of his hands in a sign of surrender. It was all I could do not to ask how much practice he'd had at making that particular gesture. "Okay, so I've been a crappy friend sometimes. I can own that. But I'm working on this whole turning over a new leaf thing." He lowered his hands and dropped his chin, giving me an earnest look. "So in the spirit of leaf-turning, let me just say...I'm happy for you. I hope it works out."

I eyed him warily, taking a moment before deciding I partway believed him. "Thanks," I said, mustering a faint smile.

"And if it doesn't work out..." Alan pulled his shoulders up in a slow shrug. "It's not like you don't have some options closer to home."

Before I'd fully processed his last statement, or the unspoken implications, Alan pushed open his door and got out. Without so much as a backward glance, he sauntered straight through his parent's yard and disappeared into one of the open garage doors. I was left with the distinct impression I wouldn't be hearing anything more from Alan unless I made a return to singleness.

*Well…that was certifiably awkward.*

Come to think of it, even my male friends online seemed to be distancing themselves as of late. Was this really how it worked? Were any of my friendships with guys real, or had I just unwittingly existed as some sort of desperate fallback plan in the event that nothing else worked out for them?

Not exactly a flattering thought.

Pulling away from the curb, I cranked up the radio and drowned out my speculating brain.

It was ten o'clock when I got home, less than an hour since Vince had called me the first time. He should have still been awake, but he wasn't picking up. I started to worry on the third try.

He'd been driving back home from Birmingham when he'd called. The commute was long, and undeniably more treacherous in the dark. Vince had kicked into volunteer firefighter mode and helped pull someone out of a flipped truck along that route less than a week before. My mind went straight to the place I didn't want it to go: picturing worst case scenarios in graphic detail. My heartbeat shot to a gallop. I waited a minute and then tried twice more in quick succession.

No one picked up.

Remembering some of the provisions I'd taken before setting out on my road trip, I hunted through my bedroom until I found the address book that held all of my primary and backup contact information. I was going to have to wake someone up.

This time, the ringing ended on the fourth round.

"H-hello?" a groggy voice half-whispered into my ear.

"Marie?" I lowered my voice, sinking onto the edge of my bed as a small fraction of my anxiety faded. "I'm so sorry to disturb you—"

"Angie?" The voice cheered with recognition.

"Yes, ma'am," I answered Vince's mother, defaulting to Southern politeness with an ease that surprised me. I hadn't spent more than a few weeks in the deep South, but more than a few parts of it had stuck with me. Marie's son, included. "Did Vincent come home tonight? He's not answering his phone. It's not like him."

"Ya know," she said, increasingly alert and not the least bit perturbed, "I thought for sure I heard the door downstairs. You just hold on a minute for me, sweetie..." I heard a rustling and a pause before she drawled, "Well, there's his car in the driveway."

My heart rate eased at the news, though the rest of me grew more perplexed. "Thank you. I just wanted to make sure he was okay."

"Vinny!" Marie's voice trilled at a muffled distance. "You sleepin' this early?

I winced. "You really don't have to—"

"Miss Angie's callin' for you." She didn't seem to hear my protest. "Are ya sick? You look like ten miles of bad road, son."

That was enough to pique my concern again. I waited a moment while some sort of shuffling handoff and incoherent exchange of muttering took place.

"Hello?" Vince's voice was beyond tired, with a tinge of something I instantly recognized as despair. I could see it in my mind's eyes as clearly as if I were able to see it on his freckled, boyish face.

"Hey, you..." I answered, scooting back on the bed until my back pressed flat to the cool drywall. "What's wrong? What happened?"

There was a long breathy pause on the other end before he spoke again. "I had...a lot of Nyquil."

"But you didn't sound sick just an hour ago," I pointed out, bewildered.

"I'm not," he said, weariness coming through clear. "I just wanted to sleep."

"You didn't want to talk to me?"

Another long beat. "I didn't think you'd get back to me tonight."

"Why wouldn't I?" Suspicion prickled at the back of my mind. "Wait...are you upset because I was hanging out with a friend tonight?"

Vince groaned. "Well, when you put it that way it sounds all controlling and psycho."

"Let me get this straight," I spoke into the phone with deliberate care. "You downed a bottle of Nyquil because you thought I blew you off?"

"Half a bottle," he amended, trading the misery in his tone for the beginnings of embarrassment. "I guess...that might seem dramatic."

"That *definitely* seems dramatic," I said, my insides scrabbling for a safe emotion to settle on. For the first time in the month since I'd agreed to this relationship, a nagging uncertainty flared within me. Maybe we couldn't handle 1,000 miles of distance after all. "Vince...that was stupid. You could have hurt yourself," I said, settling on blunt exasperation. "And over what? Me hanging out with a guy I've known since we were kicking each other's shins in the third grade—and who, by the way, I have absolutely *no* attraction to."

The line was silent for so long, I began to wonder if he'd fallen back to sleep. "He was at your house…"

"Watching a movie with me AND my parents, like I told you," I said. "It's not like we were alone."

"You never mentioned him before." It was more of a weak statement than an argument.

I sighed into the receiver. "Because he wasn't really worth mentioning." I pulled my knees up to my chest and rubbed at my temple with my free hand. "What do you want to know? He called me out of the blue today wanting to catch up. I'm betting he was just bored and nobody else was willing to give him a ride anywhere. My parents were already renting a movie, so I invited him over. At least it kept him out of trouble for a few hours." I paused, searching for reassuring words while still wondering if I was facing a huge relationship red flag. "We're not even that close. He's one of the many guys who turned me down when I was looking for somebody to go with me to my senior Prom. Even just as friends."

"Well then, he's an even bigger idiot than me," Vince said.

"I'm not debating that," I tried to keep any trace of humor out of my voice, focusing on why Vince's behavior had me rattled. "I just want to know what I've ever done that would make you think you can't trust me." My anxiety grew as I waited for Vince to respond. So, I did what I always defaulted to when I didn't know what else to do. I prayed.

*God, I need to know if this is something we can work through…or a really bad sign of things to come.*

"I'm sorry, babe," Vince said, heaving a sigh as he spoke. His usual mellow tenor returned. "I overreacted."

"Yes, yes you did," I said. His admission clung to my thoughts more than the apology. It wasn't the first time one of us had tripped over mental baggage and overreacted to the other, in some shape or form. We even had an idiom for it: "I hit a landmine, didn't I?"

It was a curious thing, this inadvertent ability to trigger unresolved issues in one another. Maybe it was just the price and privilege of caring for someone so fiercely. For better or worse, we had immediate access to each other's hearts. And I was just smart enough to grasp that along with such close emotional proximity came the potential to build, repair…or destroy.

"Alaina," Vince spoke the name of his ex-girlfriend without emotion.

I, on the other hand, bristled as though he'd just invoked an ancient curse. Understanding broadsided me. "I reminded you of her somehow?"

"A few weeks before she dumped me in that email, she started being too busy to talk when I'd call. It seemed like every other night she was in the middle of watching a movie with somebody. She was getting to know people on campus—I didn't think much of it at the time," he reflected. His voice was dull and distant. "She always told me names—acted like everything was fine."

"And, let me guess..." I said, forcing my teeth to unclench. "A couple of those names sounded familiar when you finally found out she'd been cheating on you."

"Yeah," he conceded, sullenly.

"I'm. Not. Her." I articulated each word, trying to hammer the point deep into his consciousness.

"I know."

"I will *never* be her," I pressed. Vitriol tightened my throat, creeping into my voice. "I'd rather die than hurt you that way."

"I know...I know," Vince said, as if to calm me and sort out his own awareness at the same time. "I'm sorry. You didn't do anything wrong. It was about her, not you. Just..." His voice cracked, and he took a long moment before going on. "Tell me you can forgive me for being a paranoid spaz."

He thought I was angry at *him*. That cooled me off faster than a polar swim in January.

"You're not the one I'm having trouble forgiving," I said, quieting. In that moment, I would have given almost anything to be able to touch him. "Just promise me you won't do something like that again." It was so difficult to do this — to soothe an old hurt without being able to look into those piercing green eyes and into the soul I'd come to know so well. For now, all we had were our voices. It would have to be enough.

"I won't — I promise," he said, voice strained. "I knew this would be hard. I just didn't realize it would keep getting harder the more I figure out how to love you. Twenty-two days, and I'll see you again. But right now that feels like halfway to forever."

I rested my head back against the wall and closed my eyes. I could picture him lying on the bottom bunk of his bed, staring up at nothing while running a hand through his penny-red hair. All at once, I remembered the one piece of music that had been playing on my short drive home. Maybe it was nothing, but at that instant, it struck me as too eerily significant not to mention.

"You know...I just heard a song on the radio. I hadn't heard it in a long time. It's kind of fitting, actually..."

Vince's tone dropped with alert interest. "What was it?"

I took a slow breath in. "Are You Strong Enough to Be My Man." I spoke the title matter-of-factly, without the inflection of a question.

Silence ticked away for several seconds before he spoke again—this time with conviction weighing heavy in his reply.

"I want to be."

# Ever After

–

# Part 1

You know you've been loitering somewhere too long when you start recognizing the security guards.

For the third time that afternoon I took stock of the same rotund, middle-aged man in uniform as he sauntered past my bench. He cast me a backward glance and muttered something into the walkie-talkie mic he had pinned to the inside of his shoulder. Resisting the urge to give him a friendly wave, I slid my journal into my backpack and scanned the busy Baggage Claim area of the Minneapolis airport.

Arriving two hours early was a bit excessive of me — overeager, even.

I told myself it was just prudence, given I'd never driven to the airport before and had attempted to navigate the Twin Cities just twice in the two years since receiving my driver's license. But the truth was, after a 6,000 mile road trip and traversing even larger metro areas solo, I wasn't so easily intimidated.

No, there was only one reason I was lingering about, people-watching as complete strangers collected their luggage and reunited with other complete strangers. My boyfriend's flight was coming in this afternoon. And I was stupidly, nervously, ridiculously in love.

*Boyfriend.*

The designation still sounded so foreign rolling around in my brain. Then again, I was new to this dating thing. Plus, I hadn't exactly gone about it in a way most would consider "normal."

Half an hour earlier, a thirty-something woman awaiting her ride had tried to strike up a conversation with me. "That's a lovely blouse. You look like you're waiting for someone special," she'd said, giving me a knowing smile.

I'd nodded, glancing down at the rosy, slit-sleeved peasant shirt I'd painstakingly selected for how well it fit my long, curvy frame. It was a much more feminine look than I usually attempted, but the concession was justified in my mind by the fact that I'd snagged it at a Goodwill bag sale. Deciding it wouldn't be socially acceptable to mention all this to the professional-looking woman, I volunteered what I thought she was looking for: "My boyfriend. I haven't seen him in two months."

The older blonde woman gasped. "Oh, you poor thing! That must be so difficult." With a look of intense interest she dropped to sit beside me on the bench I'd claimed, parked a little rolling suitcase at her feet, and smoothed her pencil skirt. "My fiancé travels a lot for work. They send him all over — a weekend in Vegas, a week in Japan… I can't stand it half the time, but two months?! I can't imagine."

"It's…kind of a long distance relationship," I admitted, unsure what to do with the chatty woman's attention. Should I introduce myself?

*Hi, I'm Angeli. Are you interested in becoming friends, or am I just your social life raft for the next few minutes?* I managed to contain the tactless thought. Even though, in all probability, we'd never see each other again.

Deciding the anonymity was enough reason to be my candid self, I added, "He lives in Alabama."

"Oh, well that's…quite a distance." The woman gave a lipstick-smooth smile that seemed meant to cover skepticism. "But I hear if those kinds of relationships do happen to work out, they're pretty solid. 'Whatever doesn't kill us only makes us stronger,' and all that…"

I didn't think I liked her use of the word "if," but I gave a polite smile and nodded. After all, my own family, who were well-versed in how mulishly determined I could be, was only somewhat optimistic about the potential lifespan of my first real relationship. Why should I expect more from a stranger?

As it occurred to me I should give her a turn at being the focus of discussion, the blonde woman decided to fill the silence. "I bet he's really looking forward to seeing you," she nudged my elbow with hers in a conspiratory gesture.

Guessing she was insinuating something, I tried not to look embarrassed. "I like to think so."

"How did you two meet, anyway? College? Spring break...?"

*Oh boy, here goes...*

"Technically, I guess you could say I met him on the internet," I began, noting as the woman's finely-shaped eyebrows shot up. I couldn't tell if I'd merely surprised her or if she'd just set her freak-sensors to maximum.

"But not on a matchmaking site or anything like that," I hurried on. "We started out just friends in a sort of story-writing community...thing." Specifying that it was a text-based role play game probably wouldn't help build a case for my sanity, so I left that part out. "Then I went on a road trip a few months ago to finally meet a few of my friends from there in person, and he and I just...clicked." The summary didn't do the experience any justice, but it was the best I could come up with on short notice.

"Oh," the woman uttered, shifting uncomfortably on the bench. "That's very interesting." The way she stressed the word "interesting" made me think it wasn't the term she wanted to use. At least she was polite enough to hide her bewilderment. "Were there a lot of you who went on this road trip?"

"No, it was just me," I said, impressed by how much higher her eyebrows were able to creep up her pale forehead. I was losing her. "But I was careful about it. I did background checks, self-defense training...kept a knife and a can of Mace close by. The Mace actually got me in a fair bit of trouble while I was in Canada — that's kind of a funny story..."

The woman straightened her back and craned her neck, as if tracking one of the cars passing the window through the pickup area behind us. "Oh, well, there's my ride," she said in a cheery voice. She got to her feet and shoved the rolling suitcase ahead of her. "Thanks so much for keeping me company...and good luck to you!" With a tight smile and a wave she stepped around to the automatic doors and out into the mild, late September air.

I watched her out of the corner of my eye as she paced the sidewalk for another ten minutes before a car pulled to the curb and she moved to meet it.

*Shouldn't have mentioned the knife,* I decided. I'd picked up my journal then and passed the time with a few reflections on what had brought me to this peculiar point in my life.

With my journal entry finished, I got up to check on Vincent's flight. I discovered there was still time to kill, so I made an aimless loop around the baggage carousels and through the milling crowds. The reuniting of a young couple captured my attention — if only because I couldn't miss them.

A young woman who looked just a few years older than me was coming down the escalator from her terminal, bouncing on the balls of her feet and waving. The ecstatic movement caused her head of dark, corkscrew curls to bound and recoil around her shoulders. The obvious focus of her attention was a broad-shouldered young man wearing an MSU jacket and an elated grin. He raised a hand and shuffled side to side, impatient for her to reach the ground floor. When she did, it was like a scene out of one of those romantic movies I only watched when my more idealistic friends outvoted me.

The dark-haired woman bounded into her lover's arms. He lifted her slender frame off the ground with ease, giving her a long look that struck me as entirely too private for a public place. As he lowered her back to her feet, their mouths crashed together in a dramatic display of affection. A few hoots and sighs bubbled through the crowd around them. I looked away then, feeling voyeuristic.

*And the Oscar goes to…those guys.*

I tamped down my inner sarcasm and shuffled over to an empty seat I'd spotted a few yards away. The awkward truth of the matter was…I wasn't sure what to expect when I saw Vincent. And that wasn't the first couple I'd seen set the expectation bar high.

Not that I should even consider comparing us to anyone else — our situation was as unique as it was trying. Five days. That was how long we'd spent together in person before I'd moved on to the final leg of my now infamous road trip. Vince declared his love, and I left him behind — convinced he would come to his senses. Instead he made a point to call and check on me every night. Every night we talked for hours, like two people who'd always known each other but were catching up on years we'd missed. He persisted, yet gave me enough space…until finally I stopped doing what I'd assumed was best for both of us. I stopped resisting and let myself love him. For me, there was no turning back.

Maybe I did want an earth-moving, toe-curling reunion kiss. Was that so idiotic?

I closed my eyes and settled into my newly claimed chair, blocking out the surrounding footsteps and murmurs. Quieting the usual clamor of my own mind, I hunted around for one elusive memory—struggling to recall what it had felt like when Vince and I last kissed. It shouldn't have been so difficult, but one interloping thought kept creeping in at every opportunity.

Heavy breathing...crushing weight...a dim sense of panic.

Scott.

His swarthy face and feral expression invaded my mind. I snapped my eyes open to clear the image, looking all around me at everything and nothing. A fake plant, a hobbling old man, a little boy with a teddy bear backpack... Realizing my hands were shaking, I clenched them together until they stilled in my lap. A flash of anger burned away at my anxiety.

Why did my brain keep doing this to me? Scott didn't deserve a single moment of my consideration, not anymore. It had been seven weeks since he'd irreparably shattered our friendship and my trust. And yet, he still had some insidious foothold in my mind—his betrayal haunting my thoughts and dreams. It was as though he'd left a stain on my psyche that refused to be purged.

*Oh, God...please make it go away.*

"...whatever is true, whatever is noble, whatever is right, whatever is pure, whatever is lovely, whatever is admirable...think about such things." I spoke the muddled verse under my breath, only half-aware of what I was doing. It brought me some small measure of comfort.

Vincent was noble. I knew that much as unquestionably as I knew my own name. I'd tested his resolve—not to mention his patience—time and again before ever agreeing to this relationship. In the last two months, nearly every moment he wasn't working or at college he'd spent on the phone with me. With little to cling to but each other's voices, we'd traded so many stories, hopes, and sorrows. I knew all about his dream of becoming a video game designer, and he knew every facet of my indecision over possible career paths—the endless waffling between becoming a nurse like my mother or chasing the far-fetched hope of writing for a living.

He'd listened to me fall to pieces, and he'd loved me back together. Now he was flying up to meet my parents and hopefully earn their favor.

With everything in me, I wished Vincent's was the last kiss I remembered.

The harsh blare of an alert siren snapped me out of my brooding. At the carousel across the causeway from me, a revolving red light indicated luggage was about to arrive. My gaze caught on the flight number and my heart rate kicked into a giddy double-time. A fresh mass of people were already moving down the escalator. I got to my feet and scanned each face. Finally, toward the very end of the line, I found him.

Vince's spiked, copper-colored hair stood out like a beacon. Black cargo pants and a pale blue button-up shirt did something to camouflage the leanness of his build. I'd nearly forgotten how slim he was. He was turned halfway around, having an animated conversation with someone behind him. It warmed me to watch him be sociable. He had an innate sense for people and a quickness of wit— strengths I lacked, but admired.

I stood and took a few restless steps forward, willing him to notice me.

*Wow, I'm pathetic.*

I had to marvel at myself. I couldn't recall anticipating anything with such elation and longing. Well, maybe my high school graduation, but that was like being released from prison. This being in love thing was more like looking forward to incarceration in a chocolate factory. The good European chocolate, not the waxy American variety…

Vince reached the bottom of the escalator and I forced myself to stand still. He started for the luggage carousels, pulling to almost a dead stop when he spotted me. An affected look of awe flickered across his face — keen green eyes widening behind narrow-framed glasses. Amusement tickled low in my chest as he regained his more cavalier composure and veered toward me. He didn't quicken his steps, just set his sights like I was the last level in a game he was determined to win.

Stopping toe-to-toe with me, Vince slid his laptop bag off his shoulder and set it on the floor without breaking eye contact. "Hey, Angel." A slow smile tugged at his mouth. We stood at about the same height, a few inches shy of six feet, but I had a good 40 pounds on him. Though it didn't seem to bother him, the disparity between us gave me a sudden twinge of worry.

"Hey, you," I breathed, feeling as though a small bird was thrashing around inside my ribcage. My trepidation built with every passing second. Was he going to kiss me? Should I kiss him?

*Do something, already!*

We moved at the same time, colliding into an almost desperate embrace. I tucked my chin over his shoulder and he nuzzled his smooth jaw along my neck. His clean, bar-soap smell enveloped my senses. I didn't realize how tense I'd been until I felt myself relax against him. For the first time in two months, everything seemed right.

It wasn't some Hollywood-worthy lip lock, but it was enough.

"That had to be the longest eight weeks of my life," Vince murmured in my ear.

I smiled. "I missed you, too."

After a long, relishing moment he smoothed his hands down my arms and took my hands, moving back just enough to look at me again. His eyes were as earnest as his tenor voice. "Where can we go so I can take you on a decent first date?"

I laughed. "I kind of thought our first date was when you took me to that theater in Birmingham."

"You mean the time we watched a Disney movie and I had to compete with two other guys for your attention?" Vince made a wincing face in recollection, using his thumbs to rub absent circles in the backs of my hands.

"And I still thought you were kind of a jerk?" I added, helpfully.

He smirked. "I want a do-over."

"Well, I was planning to show you the Mall of America while we're up here..."

"The biggest mall in America?" He made another pained face. "I thought you didn't like shopping."

"I don't." I smirked at his blatant discomfort. "But they have an indoor theme park...and Lego Land."

"Legos?" He perked up, a winsome smile lighting his face. His coppery brows gave an exaggerated waggle. "Now you're getting all romantic on me."

I knew that would get him. As far as I could tell, the quickest way to a geeky guy's heart usually involved geometric shapes.

I laughed. "Well, since this is the farthest you've ever been from home, I wanted to make the trip worth your while."

"You already did." Vince gave me a long, intense look. He swayed forward almost imperceptibly and then seemed to restrain himself. A charged connectivity held us for a surreal moment before he released one of my hands, grabbed up his laptop bag, and tugged me toward the baggage carousel. "Let's get out of here."

~ ~ ~ ~ ~ ~ ~

We talked nonstop all the way to the mall. As it turned out, Vince's flight had been half comprised of crew members from Cirque du Soleil. He relayed stories he'd been told by the passenger beside him, a young Quebecian woman so dedicated to the circus she'd had leopard spots tattooed all over her arms and neck.

I pretended to entertain the idea of getting the same sort of tattoos. He made a bad pun about me being a copy-cat.

"I think my dad is going to like you," I said, pulling into the first MOA parking lot I found open alongside the massive building. "He's got an unfortunate affinity for puns."

"Did you tell him I know sign language?" Vince asked.

I slowed to wait for someone backing out of a parking space and cut him a glance, sensing a setup. "No..."

"Too bad." Vince raised his arms and wriggled his fingers at me for effect. "He'd like me even more if he knew how...handy...I can be."

I thumped my forehead against the steering wheel, fighting down my own amusement. "I will leave you here," I threatened. "It's a looong walk home."

"You wouldn't make me walk," he argued. "I'd freeze to death."

I rolled my eyes and turned the wheel, swooping the car into the newly vacant parking spot. "It's almost sixty degrees right now."

"See? I knew I should have packed more than a hoodie."

I put the car in park and turned the engine off, shaking my head in mock exasperation. "Poor, poor Southern boy..." I unclicked my seatbelt as I pivoted toward him and stopped, caught off guard by the seriousness in his eyes. He leaned toward me. The slight lift to the corners of his mouth—and the fact that he'd slipped his glasses off—told me he was done talking about the weather.

So was I.

We came together at the same time in a zealous tangle of senses. Vince's lips covered mine, deft fingers caressing my jaw and threading through the long hair on either side of my face. I slid my hands over his shoulders and grappled to him like a lifeline, my mouth sparring with his. It was as if we were racing to convey what words would never entirely express.

I was only vaguely aware when he pulled me out of my seat and sidelong across his lap. He managed to do so with surprising ease, and without pause or interruption. When we slowed, it was to a savoring pace, nibbling and searching. Searching for what, I didn't know. I was so elated by our closeness it overwhelmed every corner of my mind.

His hands kneaded my back and I sighed. He answered with a low, almost pained sound. It was enough to send my wits rushing back to me. I pulled away and set my chin on his shoulder. We were both still for a few silent moments, catching our breath. As my perception funneled outward I forced my toes to uncurl and smiled to myself. He hadn't just jogged my memory; he'd overwritten every previous kiss in my brief history of kissing.

"Sorry," he murmured. "I couldn't wait anymore."

I turned my head to look at him, still resting comfortably against his chest. From there I took in every detail of his stately profile—from the striking bright eyes and dusting of freckles that made him look so much younger than the old-soul nineteen I knew him to be…to his straight, hawkish nose and almost unfairly generous lips. "You're not sorry," I accused, keeping my voice light and teasing. It had the intended effect. He formed a slow smile, gaze cutting my way before the rest of his face followed. "And I don't know what you were waiting for."

Vince chuckled at that, eyes flickering to look out the windshield and then back at me. "I've never been a big fan of public displays of affection. Always seemed like a cry for attention."

I followed his gaze toward the entrance of the mall and realized we had an audience. A plump, elderly woman with a head full of white curls had stopped on the sidewalk and stood glowering in our general direction. *Oh.* Not for the first time in my life, I thanked God I wasn't prone to blushing.

Turning back, I hid my face against his shoulder. "We just made out in my car...in front of the Mall of America," I said in quiet disbelief.

"Yep," he said, tone void of remorse but carrying the first hint of a drawl I'd ever heard from him. "We sure did." His fingers traced enticing, feather-light trails up and down my arm. "I'm up for round two, if you are..."

I lifted my head and gave his shoulder a swat. "I'm up for going inside before somebody calls mall security on us."

He grinned at me, his eyes crinkling at the corners in a roguish way that almost changed my mind. "Whatever makes you happy, babe."

~ ~ ~ ~ ~ ~ ~

Our do-over "first date" went better than I could have hoped.

After we tired of studying Lego sculptures and walking around the enormous mall complex until our feet were sore, Vince took me to dinner at an Italian restaurant I knew he couldn't afford. He looked wounded when I only ordered an appetizer, but I convinced him I wasn't especially hungry.

It was the truth at least. Being around him threw me off in almost every absurd way I'd read about in countless books, but never experienced before meeting him. I couldn't quite decide if I should be thrilled or terrified by the fact. Thrilled because it was so new to me; terrified because it couldn't last. Like a supernova, nothing this intense could burn so bright indefinitely. The question was, what would be left between us once the newness wore off?

That gnawing uncertainty was enough to keep my stomach unsettled. After all, there were only two fated outcomes for a supernova: a stable, luminous neutron star…or a sucking black hole.

"So…did you ask your parents about where I'll be sleeping?" Vince asked as we started out the hour-long drive south down highway 169. He'd claimed my right hand, threading our fingers together and resting them against the edge of the passenger seat. It was everything I could do to split my attention between driving, talking, and being compellingly aware of the subtle slide of our connected fingers.

"You mean…about asking if you could sleep on the floor in my bedroom?" My stomach did a somersault. "Yeah, I ran it past them. They weren't happy." I shook my head, resisting the urge to glance his way.

"I swear I'm not going to try anything," he said, voice tinged with disappointment. "I only get to see you for nine days. I just…want to be close to you for as much of that as I can get."

"I know." I squeezed his hand, chewing the inside of my lower lip in nervous frustration. "And I feel the same way. I promised them we'd behave, but the problem isn't so much about trust…" I finally ventured a glance at his intent face. The sun had begun to set, backlighting his hair with a fiery orange-gold glow. "It's about my younger sister and brother. I'm supposed to be setting some sort of example for them. If my parents let you have a sleepover in my bedroom—"

"—they couldn't tell your siblings they're not allowed to do the same thing without being hypocritical." Vince grumbled the revelation with an air of resignation.

"And Bingo was his name-O." I nodded.

"Maybe being an only child isn't so bad."

I chuckled. "Maybe not."

He stared ahead for a long moment, brows furrowed in deep thought. "Are your parents mad at me for asking?"

"Well, I think my mom understood..." Hesitating, I poured more of my focus into driving. Around us the Twin Cities' suburbs waned into a small-town feel, broken up by patchy fields and strips of forest.

"And your dad?"

"He might have looked a little...angry," I confessed. In my mind's eye I recalled the tense set of my father's jaw, the way his sandy brows pulled low over his piercing blue eyes. Yes, definitely angry. But not a spittle-flying rage, at least. He hadn't had one of those since his heart attack almost a full year past.

Vince shifted in his seat. "Does your dad happen to...I don't know...own any guns?" His tone reached for joking but didn't quite make it.

"A few of them," I answered, stifling a snigger when I felt Vince's arm go rigid. "He's not going to shoot you. He probably won't even bring them out for a passive-aggressive cleaning. I think that's reserved for when my little sister brings boyfriends around. I'm the tough, careful one who's not supposed to need protecting."

"Right. You're the one who got in her car and drove around the continent for eight weeks," Vince pointed out. "Alone. Visiting weirdoes you met on the internet."

"Says weirdo number ten," I countered.

He laughed—a light, comforting sound that made me feel accomplished. "Touché."

"You know, my dad did say something about having you sleep in the playhouse," I said as the recollection hit me. "But I *think* he was just joking."

"Playhouse?" Vince cocked a skeptical eyebrow. "That conjures images of a giant dollhouse in your living room. I gotta say, I'm not loving that idea."

I shook my head. "It's...hard to explain. It's more like a tree-house, but it's not in a tree."

"He wants to keep me outside? In a tree fort?!" Dramatized horror crept into his voice, raising it an octave. "I take it back. I'd rather sleep in the dollhouse."

"There's no dollhouse." I laughed, finding it difficult to keep my focus on the road. "Don't worry about it. My dad's been mostly bark and no bite since he recovered from his heart attack."

"Your dad is a disgruntled postal worker with a gun collection—" Vince stressed, leaning to close the gap between us. "—and two beautiful daughters." His voice lowered with a blend of amusement and sincerity. I couldn't help it when heat crept up my neck in response to his nearness. "Sorry, but I think I'll err on the side of worry."

I pondered pulling the car over and obeying the impulse to kiss him. I wasn't the best driver even in distraction-free conditions, and right at that moment, my mood was bordering on reckless endangerment. Fortunately, we were approaching an attention-commanding landmark.    Valleyfair rose up along the right side of the highway, its winding roller-coasters and colorful rides sprawling out in a dense backdrop of entertainment options. Beside me Vince uttered a low "whoa" as a 180-foot Skycoaster ride catapulted a set of harnessed people in our direction.

"We used to come here once every summer," I said, watching out of the corner of my eye as the thrill-seekers reached the end of their tether and swung back toward the amusement park like a pendulum. "That's the RipCord. I've always wanted to try that thing. It costs a little extra, but it'd be worth it to cross bungee-jumping off my list."

"You have a bucket list?" Vince sounded surprised.

"Well, sort of." I shrugged. "It's not so much a list of things I want to do before I die. More like…a directory of experiences I'd like to have before I try to get serious about writing."

Vince was silent for a few seconds. I thought he was about to tease me for being overly analytical, but instead when he spoke it was in all seriousness, "We could stop. If you want to check that off your list now, I'll go with you."

I smiled. "That's really sweet of you, Vincent." I glanced aside at him, keeping the car on course for home. "And kind of insane, considering you have a problem with heights."

"I don't have a problem with them, they have a problem with me," he said, smirking. "Seriously, I'm up for facing my fears today."

"Are you sure you're not just putting off meeting my dad?"

"Probably." He grinned. "Okay, so some fears are worse than others. But I mean it. If you want an experience, I want to give it to you." He tightened his hold on my hand, and I wondered how deep his meaning went before his grin widened. "I just can't promise I'll keep my eyes open."

I thought about it.

My last chance for an exit and easy turn-around was coming up, and the idea of sharing such an exhilarating venture with him was tempting. But the practical side of me was stronger. "The line is probably long, and it'll be dark soon. I don't want to drive the rest of the way back at night—too many suicidal deer on this road." With a sidelong glance I caught the look of relief on his face. "Besides, I haven't updated my last will and testament since before the road trip. I should probably do that before I take any more unnecessary risks."

"You have a will?" The shock in Vince's voice was enough to earn him the longest glance I dared give. He didn't have much color to begin with, but what he did have had gone into hiding. It was as though the idea of me having a will scared him more than heights and my father combined. "Why? What eighteen-year-old just…decides to write out their will?"

*And here I thought he'd gotten used to my oddness.*

"An eighteen-year-old who's almost died before?" I offered, keeping my voice soft. I fixed my gaze on the highway ahead, putting extra concentration into passing a slow SUV towing an oversized speedboat. "I know I've mentioned that whole run-over-by-a-truck incident I had when I was twelve. Ever since then I've just...had a really solid awareness of my own mortality. I think about it almost every day." I pulled my shoulders into a shrug. With the slight shift in movement I noted his hand was cool and clammy. I flexed my fingers and tried to disentangle them from his, but he moved with me instead of releasing his hold.

"And anyway," I went on, uneasy with his evident discomfort. "It's not like it's a legal document. I don't have much to leave behind. It's just a file on my computer — something to say what I want to say, and hopefully inconvenience people as little as possible."

"You think about your death a lot," Vince reiterated at last. From his tone I couldn't tell if he was more baffled or appalled. "And you think about keeping it from being an *inconvenience* to people?"

"Okay, when you put it that way it sounds kind of morbid," I admitted, forcing a small chuckle. I glanced at his face and couldn't find a trace of his usual good-humor. The approach of dusk sent shadows playing across his sharp cheekbones, giving his eyes a raw look of distress. "Oh, hey, no..." Clumsy words bubbled up to reassure him. "I'm not saying I *want* to die. I mean, I might have once...but it's been a long time since I've had thoughts like that. Years. I'm okay now."

*Good grief, I'm making it worse.*

"Really, I mean it." I tried again. My emotions roiled, rivaling the dips and curves of the roller coasters we'd left behind. "I know I probably seem a little unstable sometimes...especially for two or three days out of the month...but I don't want you to think—"

He lifted my hand and pressed the backs of my knuckles to his lips. Everything in me went quiet.

"I don't think you're unstable," he said finally. "I'm just...not ready to think about you dying. That's all."

My heart gave a few heavy thumps. "Sorry," I said, keeping my eyes on the road ahead. "Sometimes I forget how I think about things isn't exactly...typical."

"Well, I didn't fly up here because I thought you were typical." With another sidelong glance I noticed his face ease into a pensive smile. "I remember you mentioning the near-death thing, but I think you just summarized. Are you going to tell me the whole story?"

I searched my memory for a good starting point. "I suppose we do have some travel time to kill."

# Girl vs. Truck

It was a warm day, I remember. A Friday afternoon in early May, and my sixth grade school year would be over in just a few weeks. I had taken off on my bike for a brief after-school excursion.

As I often did, I had ridden my bike halfway around the circular subdivision that made up our neighborhood. The area was still undeveloped, with large stretches of forest wedged between most of the recently built houses. I can still recall how much my angsty younger self enjoyed abandoning civilization. I would spend countless hours in those woodsy areas, amusing myself with archery and building wigwam forts.

On that particular day I must have stayed out too long, because my younger brother and sister eventually came looking for me. I was irritated at being disturbed, but they claimed my father had sent them out to find me. I had a babysitting job that evening and he didn't want me to be late.

Begrudgingly, I pulled my black BMX dirt bike out of the tangle of wild raspberry bushes I'd parked it in for safekeeping. True, it was technically a boy's bike. But being a tomboy, I regarded it as my pride and joy.

I rode ahead of my siblings for the half-mile ride back. Pedaling hard, I felt a vague satisfaction in being able to outpace them.

As I neared our gravel driveway I began to coast down the incline. I stood up on the pedals and watched the trees fly past as a green blur in my peripheral vision, enjoying the last leg of the ride. To my right, a large tree had bushed out to effectively block my view of anything down that particular branch of the four-way intersection I was fast approaching.

At that moment, something was coming down that road — and in a treacherous hurry.

Unfortunately for me, that something happened to be a bright blue pickup truck towing a flatbed trailer. Secured atop that trailer was a backhoe loader. The steady crunching of my bike tires over the gravel had camouflaged the sound of the oncoming vehicle. I had only a second to react as the nose of the pickup appeared from behind the tree, and I realized we were about to collide.

I stomped back on my brakes, but my bike just kept sliding forward over the loose rocks and dust. My perception of time seemed to slow, as though I'd become my own helpless spectator. I suppose I was in shock at that point, grasping the fact that what was about to happen was totally beyond my control.

I didn't have time to be afraid.

I remembered the jarring thud that came when I careened into the driver's side door of the vehicle. I got a brief glimpse of the stunned middle-aged driver as the front wheel of my bike was sucked underneath his truck. I felt myself pitching forward to join the fate of my bicycle, but then my body suddenly lurched—in a sensation like someone had grabbed me around the waist and yanked me backward. Then I began to fall, dropping onto the gravel road, never feeling any sort of impact as I landed flat on my back. I saw the light blue of the sky above and heard nothing but the low roar of the truck as it devoured my dirt bike.

I've heard many accounts of people who've been through a trauma stating they "blacked out" for a short time. I guessed I was having a similar occurrence as I was laid out on my back with the trailer grinding past me. Except what I experienced was quite the opposite. I was enveloped in a bright, calm whiteness. It felt warm, safe and serene; almost like being hugged.

My ten-year-old sister later filled me in on what she saw after I'd fallen on my back. She and my younger brother managed to stop their bikes several yards short of the accident, watching as my legs remained straight up in the air as the rest of the truck and the first set of trailer tires sped by. According to her my legs then dropped to the ground, where they were both run over by the last set of tires.

I didn't perceive things in quite the same way.

I know in my mind that this all happened very fast, but being in the midst of it, time was hard to gauge. I never lost awareness. My hearing became dull and muffled, as though I'd been encased in cotton. The whiteout persisted and I could sense the trailer rolling past me. I felt two dull *thumps* reverberate through my body when the tires ran over my calves. I felt no pain while it was happening, just pressure accompanied by an odd tingling sensation.

The whiteness faded away and I found myself sitting up in the middle of the intersection, looking at the back of the trailer as the truck finally managed to stop some fifteen or twenty yards further down the road.

All at once I became conscious of a heavy ache settling into my calves. I was also acutely aware that my sister was screaming — a shrieking, horrified sound I'd never heard before. I saw her standing with my brother a short ways up the hill I'd just careened down. They both dropped their bikes and came running toward me, yelling. It took a moment to process their words, but I realized they were asking if I was okay. I only managed to grit my teeth and inform them that I thought my legs were broken.

The dumbfounded truck driver stepped out and called back to me asking the same question. I just shook my head, trying not to concentrate on the increasingly throbbing pain. The driver seemed afraid to walk toward me, which was fine. I wasn't particularly happy with him.

By this time our lifelong neighbor, Charles — whose house was across the road from the tree that had blocked my view—heard the commotion and came bounding out of his workshop. Charles was a heavyset Italian man, and I recall being surprised by how fast he crossed his yard to reach me. While he bent to assess my injuries, my sister ran the rest of the way home to find my dad. I answered Charles' questions in monosyllables amid my painful daze. I told myself not to focus on anything, convinced that if I concentrated at all, the pain would be much worse.

Moments later my dad came tearing out of our long driveway in his tiny white sedan, nearly backing over the mailbox in the process. He scooped me up like I weighed nothing and deposited me in the passenger seat. I had been wearing jeans, so my injuries weren't yet visible. Still, he was more distraught than I'd ever seen him as he sped back up the driveway.

By the time we'd parked in the garage I had more of my wits about me. Despite the bone-deep aching in my calves, I stubbornly refused help as I managed to stand and hobble into the house. I'd decided that if I could walk at all, it must mean I wasn't hurt as bad as I thought. There was still a chance I could make it to my babysitting job later that evening. Maybe if I just stayed on the couch and kept my feet up, I could tough it out.

When I got to the bathroom, I finally accepted I wouldn't be babysitting anyone but myself.

A nickel-sized puncture wound plunged deep into the side of my left kneecap—likely caused by some sharp chunk of gravel. The wound was bleeding steadily, already trickling down to soak my sock and pool in my shoe. Gruesome layers of skin, fat, and cartilage were visible through the hole and I had no feeling at all for about two inches around the wound. The strange lack of sensation was almost worse than pain.

The back of my right calf bore two deep abrasions down the length of it. The imprint of tire tread marks were already turning purple across both of my swelling calves and shins.

After calling my mother at work, my dad opted to take me to the emergency room. I didn't like that idea, but I couldn't see any way out of it. I needed more than a band-aid and no amount of stubbornness was going to help the fact.

Once we got to the hospital I was stitched up, drugged up, and had multiple x-rays taken. Remarkably, though I'd fallen onto rough gravel, my injuries were confined to my legs. The back of my shirt wasn't torn or even dirty.

A stern-looking policeman asked me to recount what happened, and I recited back everything to him exactly as I'd perceived it—from the tree blocking my view, to the whiteout experience, to my father having to carry me as he sprinted through the emergency room leaving a trail of blood drops behind us. When I mentioned feeling like someone had grabbed me and pulled me backward off of my bike, the officer's bushy eyebrows bunched together like warring caterpillars. I was pretty sure he didn't believe me. Thanks in part to the wondrous powers of modern medicine, I really didn't care.

At one point I overheard a doctor mentioning that if my calves continued to swell, they might have to slit my skin open from knee to ankle to allow more room for the muscle tissue to distend. That possibility had me panicky and considering all possible escape routes for a couple of hours. Fortunately, it didn't come to that.

The x-ray results eventually came back and, much to everyone's surprise, I had no broken bones. I would be hobbling for several weeks with severe tire tread-shaped contusions hidden under Ace Bandages, but my recovery time was minimal, all things considered. I spent the next several days in a near-giddy state of astonishment over my continued existence.

It's hard to look at life the same when you've had a close brush with death. Or at least, that much was true for me. I've thought back on that day countless times, and I still find it amazing. Whether anyone else believes it or not, I'm convinced that God protected me. The scars may not be pretty, but they're a part of me. An ever-present reminder I wouldn't remove even if I could. In some of my darkest hours, the recollection of that incident had always been pulled to the forefront of my mind.

And along with it, the quiet assurance that I'm alive for a reason.

# Ever After
-
# Part 2

"Wait...so you got run down by a truck, and you didn't even get out of school for it?" Vince picked out the one piece of my harrowing tale he'd apparently found the most disturbing.

His selective incredulity made me laugh. "I didn't have any broken bones, and nobody thought to ask the emergency room doctor for a note. So yeah, I went back to school that Monday."

In the time it took me to relay the story and answer his questions, we'd made it to my hometown. Just big enough to warrant a handful of small tech schools and a branch of the State University, the city sprawled out along the bluffs and plains on either side of the Minnesota River. It took only ten minutes to cut straight through to the outskirts. I drove the route on mental auto-pilot, my thoughts lingering somewhere with my angsty twelve-year-old self.

"Going back to school wasn't so bad," I went on. "Until people started asking why I was limping."

"What, they didn't think it was awesome you survived something like that?"

"Hardly anybody believed me." I gave a small shrug, noting his sober expression out of the corner of my eye. "I unwrapped part of my leg—showed them the bruises. But most of the kids in my class just laughed and thought it was fake. They said it didn't make sense for something like that to happen and my legs not end up broken. Even some of the teachers thought I was exaggerating...trying to get attention or something."

"What's so hard to believe?" Vince asked, sounding a touch riled. "It's not like you claimed you'd sprouted wings and orchestrated world peace." His sarcastic indignation warmed me to the core, soothing the old pang of rejection I barely knew I'd been nursing.

"No, but I was weird. I guess that was enough to make me a liar too." I shook my head, as if it would shake off the memory. "I asked my mom if we could get a copy of my medical files so I could bring them to school and prove how bad I was hurt...but she said it wasn't worth it. 'If people want to believe—or disbelieve—something, they'll always find a reason to.'" I drew quotes for the mom-ism with one hand while keeping the other on the steering wheel. "I was mad at her back then, but now I'm pretty sure she was right."

Vince assembled an inventive string of curses under his breath. I reached aside and patted his knee, the gesture half calming and half appreciative.

"Well, here we are." I motioned as my car crested a familiar hill. The woods-lined valley below held several dozen unremarkable homes spaced unevenly around and between two branching gravel roads. "Home sweet home, for the whole last eighteen years of my life."

"Cozy," Vince said, leaning to survey the partially lit valley from his window. He pushed his glasses up the bridge of his nose with a casual flick of his middle and index finger. There was no reason I should find the habit endearing, but for some reason I did. "Must have been nice growing up around here. Well, nicer than growing up on prison grounds, probably," he said, a smirk in his voice as he referenced his unorthodox childhood as the son of a State Penitentiary worker.

"Maybe not." I frowned, inwardly examining a sudden surge of caustic emotions. "At least you had some friends. Inmates your dad trusted, cousins your age...that neighbor kid you played Dungeons and Dragons with."

Whenever I saw the forking mouth to the neighborhood where I'd once caught the school bus each morning, I couldn't help but remember the taunting, hair-pulling, and snowdrift swirlies that defined my elementary and middle school years. Humiliation ran deep.

Halfway through the lower valley sat a plain, two-story house with yellow shutters—home to a pair of sisters who'd pretended to befriend me when I was eleven. I'd walked them home from the bus stop every day for a week, excited that I finally had someone to play with after school. But when I brought over my pet salamanders to show them one Saturday, they'd screamed in disgust and called over a crowd of neighborhood kids. I should have run home. Instead, I took out one of my amphibian friends and tried to demonstrate how gentle and harmless they were. And while I was distracted, the older sister dumped the rest of the salamanders down the back of my pants.

On the far right side of the valley was a cylindrical drainage culvert where two of the older neighborhood boys once cornered me—hurling rocks into both ends when I wouldn't come out to face their torment. I still recalled the throbbing sting when one of those rocks struck my face and split my upper lip. "I tried making friends around here. It just never worked for me."

At least the kids in my neighborhood had taught me one thing: better to face your fears head-on than risk them throwing stones when you're at your most vulnerable. I'd carried that lesson with me when I decided to go on my post-high school road trip. And facing that fear, the fear of braving the world alone, had brought me to Vincent.

"So, then what did you used to do for fun around here?" Vince asked. He turned his gaze back to me, seeming to pick up on my reminiscence-induced melancholy. "I mean, besides building wigwams in the woods and getting run over by heavy machinery."

"Smart-aleck," I accused, cutting him a narrowed glance. He cracked a rascally grin and waited, his lean face smoothing into a look of expectation.

I gestured further down the country highway, pointing out the glint of a roadside stream as I turned into my neighborhood. "I spent most of my time following that creek to the river with an ice-cream bucket and a butterfly net, catching crayfish and tadpoles. They weren't much for conversation, but they were more pleasant company than the kids around here."

He peered at me as the car bumped and jostled along the gravel, heading through the elevated left side of the valley. "And...what did you do with these buckets full of water creatures?"

"I kept them in a kiddie pool under our deck," I answered, matter-of-factly.

He nodded, making no attempt to mask his perplexed expression. "Oh, of course you did."

A small smirk leaked through, tugging at the side of my mouth he couldn't see. "Some girls took dance or played with dolls... I created an aquatic ecosystem in my backyard."

"Well," He cleared his throat, playing up a tone of confused acquiescence. "Everybody needs a hobby."

I turned left into a small cul-de-sac and eased into park in front of my parent's house. Painted dark blue and set on a small plateau, it would have blended into the darkened woods behind it if not for the motion-sensing floodlights and glaring-white garage doors. I switched off the engine and turned to look Vince full in the face.

"Last chance to back out," I offered with forced cheer, taking in a steadying breath as he leaned toward me. "There's probably a lot more weirdness from here on out—"

Vince bent forward the rest of the way and captured my lips in a sweet, lingering kiss. His hand cupped my jaw, giving gentle guidance as I mirrored his movements without thought. He pulled back first, lips curving into a smile of challenge.

"Bring on the weird."

~ ~ ~ ~ ~ ~ ~

The first member of my family to meet Vincent was Hale-Bopp, our five-year-old mutt of a dog. She greeted us in the entryway and submitted her approval by flopping belly-up onto his feet.

"As you can see, she's quite vicious," I quipped, smiling as Vince crouched low and gave the animal a thorough tummy rub, complete with ear massage and crooning compliments. I expected as much, given the affection I'd seen him display for his Miniature Pinscher, Budweiser. Compared to that obstinate sausage-with-legs, Hale-Bopp was the doggie equivalent of a saint.

"What kind of mix is she?" Vince asked as he finally stood, having secured complete adoration from both me and Haley.

"Half Border Collie, half sneaky neighbor dog." I shrugged and bent to scratch between Haley's partially-raised ears. She was a perfect medium-size, extra fluffy, with cinnamon and white markings. "That's what the ad in the paper said, anyway. My mom wanted a Collie. Dad didn't want a dog in the first place, so he definitely didn't want to spend money on one. And I was so happy to finally get a puppy, I didn't care if she was off-brand."

Vince raised a coppery eyebrow, following me inside to the stairwell landing of our split-level home. His shoulder brushed mine as he stepped out of his shoes and glanced around. "And where did her name come from? ...not that I'm making any judgments about pet names."

I laughed. "Mom's idea. Well, okay, my obsession with outer space probably influenced her a little. That was the year of the comet Hale-Bopp. The evening we adopted her we could see it on the horizon, and —"

"Ah!" An exuberant cry came from somewhere upstairs. Joelle, my spritely sixteen-year-old sister, came dashing from somewhere near the kitchen and stopped just short of charging down the carpeted steps. Her silken, honey-brown hair billowed about her face in long waves before settling. "The invisible boyfriend is real!"

"And...this is my little sister," I offered, making a sweeping hand motion in introduction before stage-whispering, "She thought you were just an excuse for me to be on the computer all the time."

"Hogging the computer, you mean. And the phone." Joelle pursed her pouty lips, topaz-blue eyes narrowed in passing annoyance. Her gaze flit from me to Vince and her countenance brightened. "You got here just in time for dinner. Dad decided to go hunting out at grandma's, so now Mom's making crock pot barbeque squirrel." She scrunched up her nose in obvious distaste and lowered her voice to a conspiratorial level. "I'm having cereal."

Part of me hoped she was being funny, but odds were good she wasn't joking. As the youngest of eight children from an impoverished rural family, my dad had never quite shaken a rustic sort of "waste not, want not" mentality. It showed up in everything from his sizable weapons collection, to the wood-burning stove we used to heat our house, to his longtime side job as a gopher bounty hunter. My mother tolerated and occasionally humored his frontiersman eccentricities.

Up until recently, I'd regarded these quirks as a normal part of life. But after spending the summer with ten very different families from across the continent, I was more convinced than ever that "normal" was just some manufactured illusion of consensus. Sort of like mass hysteria…but in reverse.

*Mass normalcy.* Now there was a dismal concept.

"Squirrel for dinner," Vincent repeated, raising skeptical brows at me from behind his narrow-framed glasses.

"Marinated tree rat." I tapped the end of his nose and smiled. "Just remember, I gave you every chance to back out."

"Aww," Joelle crooned. She formed the shape of an L with each of her thumbs and forefingers, holding them out to create a frame around her line of sight. "You two look adorable together. Oh! How about I take some couples photos for you guys sometime this week?"

I started to protest on reflex, but then realized there weren't any pictures of Vince and I together yet. Tangible evidence of our togetherness seemed appealing. "You know…that would actually be really great." I smiled and glanced at Vince. "You okay with that?"

"I don't mind…" Vince whipped off his glasses in an over-dramatized motion, cocked his head, and raised an eyebrow in my sister's general direction. "As long as she gets my good side."

I palmed my face.

My sister bounced on the balls of her feet and clapped, looking thoroughly delighted. "Oh, I like him already."

Vince held up a hand to hide his mouth and stage-whispered aside to me, "That's one down. How many more family members do I have to impress?"

I smirked at him and looked up the steps to my sister. "I'm guessing Mom's busy cooking. Where's Dad?"

"He was downstairs, last time I saw him." Joelle tossed her hair over one shoulder and combed through it with her fingers, shrugging. "Don't worry. He had more than just his underwear on."

I winced in vague discomfort and pivoted toward the descending half of the staircase, not venturing to gauge Vince's reaction. "I hadn't even thought to worry about that until you mentioned it. Thanks, sis."

"Any time, sis." Joelle smiled broadly. She wiggled her fingers at us in a cutesy wave, then turned and flounced back toward the dining room.

I headed to the basement to get the rest of the tour over with. At the base of the steps I pointed out our bedrooms in brief, starting with my sister's to the immediate right. Her door was standing open, leaving her fairyland/dolphin theme on display. My room was the second door down, and I was relieved it was closed. Outer space and wolves suddenly seemed like juvenile choices in décor.

My younger brother's room was straight ahead — more of a converted closet space, with a tiny window and walls lined with video game paraphernalia. He wasn't in his room, so I banked left into the L-shaped den.

Vince gravitated to the brick-lined alcove in one corner, where the boxy wood-burning stove radiated a steady aura of warmth. He stepped onto the bricks and held out his hands toward the orange glow of the glass-faced door. "Nice," he said, giving me a sidelong smirk. "I think I found my favorite spot."

"Not quite," I said, looping an arm through the crook in his elbow and leading him around the bend to the open space we used as an office. Two desks lined the wall to the right. I gestured to an empty folding table along the left wall beside a black mini fridge. "You can set up your laptop here, if you want. The fridge is stocked with all things caffeinated."

"You know me well," Vince said, appreciation tingeing his voice.

I motioned with my chin to indicate my fifteen-year-old brother, who sat transfixed at one of the two computer stations our household shared. "I'm pretty sure you and Tyler will get along just fine."

In a belated response to hearing his name, Tyler pulled his headphones down to rest on his shoulders and looked up from the vampire game he'd been enthralled with. "What, now?" He blinked at me, and then raised a hand in standard greeting when he registered Vince's presence. "Hey, man."

Tyler, like me, pulled his appearance from my mother's side of the gene pool. Long-limbed and taller than average, he somehow managed an athlete's build despite avoiding anything that vaguely resembled sports. He was dark-featured, with a head full of thick espresso-colored hair—which he kept just long enough to sculpt into a helmet-like coif that resembled some character out of a Japanese cartoon. If not for the awkward beginnings of a spindly moustache, he might have looked closer to Vince's age.

I made a sweeping gesture of introduction. "Ty, this is Vince. Vince...Tyler."

The guys nodded at each other. I relaxed my hold on Vince, and he stepped up to peer at the paused computer screen. "I haven't played this one in a while. Level twenty-three?"

My brother raised his brows in a pleasantly surprised look. "Yeah, I'm still working out the puzzle on this one. I don't like using walkthroughs—seems too much like cheating."

"Same here." Vince nodded, scanning through a stack of games beside the computer.

I smiled to myself as they worked up an easy conversation centered around their tastes in gameplay and animation styles. I started to follow along, but my attention drifted to the doorway of the utility room at the back right side of the office. The door stood half open and the light was on. Reasonably sure I'd located my dad, I walked over and peeked in.

I was met with what looked like the scene of a mass murder. A narrow table was set up in the cramped space, the freshly-skinned carcasses of two grey squirrels laid out in the middle beside an ice cream bucket full of bloodied water. Dad stood at the far end over a freezer bag full of meat, gingerly picking fur off the end of something that resembled a small chicken drumstick—or it would have, if I didn't know better.

Dad looked up from his morbid work and smiled. A short, stocky man with sandy hair and pale eyes, it occurred to me that most wouldn't find him particularly imposing—except for the fact that his fingers were currently coated in blood. "Hey, sweetie. Made it back from the airport okay?"

"Yeah...no problems," I said, trying not to make eye contact with the dismembered head of a fox squirrel I'd just noticed facing my end of the table. The creatures were devastatingly cute while alive and, despite years of exposure, I still couldn't fully stomach the guilt of seeing them reduced to a future entrée. "Any particular reason you picked today to cull the squirrel population?"

"I had the day off," he answered, taking my question as curious rather than accusatory. "And they've been getting into the bird feeders so much lately, your grandmother hasn't been able to watch her favorite finches."

"Ah," I said, calming by several degrees. "I guess they won't make that mistake again."

Okay, so maybe he wasn't deliberately trying to spook Vince. The great Squirrel vs. Finch wars had been raging for years now, and it wasn't unusual for my dad to go out of his way to do things to help my grandmother.

Dad's voice was amiable and unassuming, "Well, where's this boyfriend of yours? I'd like to meet him," he said, tucking the "drumstick" into the freezer bag before dipping his bloody fingers in the bucket of water. The dichotomy of the whole thing struck me as darkly comical.

"He's...here." I eased back a step and grabbed the doorknob. "How about you clean up the crime scene and meet him upstairs? It sounds like dinner is about ready, anyway..." Feeling a warm presence at my back I startled, jerking the door closed as I spun to face Vincent. He stood almost nose-to-nose with me, a perplexed look of amusement lighting his face.

"Your dad in there?"

"Yeah," I said, making a dismissive motion with one hand. I wasn't sure if the heat rising up my neck was due to our sudden closeness, or the sight I was trying to spare him from. "He's...kinda busy. Let's go find my mom—see if she needs help with setting the table." I took his arm and steered him back through the den.

"O—kay?" Vince relented with little more than a wondering look.

~ ~ ~ ~ ~ ~ ~

Dinner went along just as most evening meals did in my family. We all sat around the oval dinner table, passing side dishes and taking turns humoring Mom with summaries of our day. Joelle went into lively detail in her usual animated tones, while Tyler spoke as little as possible at a low mutter.

It didn't take long for my first-impression worries to ease. Vincent settled into the family dynamic with an effortlessness that surprised me, considering how foreign we must have seemed to him. I knew in his family, dinner time consisted of TV trays and Vince keeping up the solitary tradition of taking his food to his room. If he was at all uncomfortable, it didn't show. He accepted a piece of barbequed squirrel without balking and managed to keep up genial conversation. My mother shared a wince-worthy nursing anecdote about a patient she'd had recently, and Vince offered a humorously gruesome story about one of the car accident calls he'd answered while volunteering for the fire department.

The entire time, Vince kept his knee pressed to mine under the table—a warm and constant point of contact. I wasn't sure if it was meant to reassure me or him.

By the end of the meal my dad looked contentedly relaxed, and I had the strong suspicion that Vince was winning my mother over.

"Do you have something against peas, Vincent?" my mother asked, motioning across the table to his nearly empty plate with a flick of her fork.

Vince's eyes widened, his gaze darting side to side as though he were looking for assistance. "Ma'am?"

Mom's dark brows lifted, disappearing under her equally dark bangs as she gave him a knowing smile. I knew that look—it was the same she used when my siblings and I were younger and she'd caught us trying to get away with something. She extended her arm and hooked her fork under the picked-clean ribcage on Vince's plate, lifting it. A full helping of peas spilled out from under their boney hiding place.

"Busted," Joelle snickered to my right.

"Oh...so *that's* where those went," Vince said, voice jumping an octave as he feigned amazement. He made a show of shuffling the pile of tiny spheres around his plate.

"He doesn't really like vegetables," I piped up lamely in his defense. I couldn't decide if I was more entertained or embarrassed. As silly as it was, I was fairly sure I'd just suffered a minor setback in my efforts to convince everyone that my baby-faced boyfriend was — in fact — exceptionally mature for his age.

"Why did you take them if you didn't want them?" Mom asked, scrutinizing Vince with a look that fell somewhere between perplexed and amused.

"Well, I didn't want to be rude." Vince formed a sheepish half-smile. "And if you're looking for full disclosure here...I guess I was counting on Haley to help me out. She turned out to be a lot pickier than my dog." He bent aside then and addressed Haley where she laid under the table. "Thanks for nothing, by the way."

His tone of mock betrayal got all of the women in my family laughing. "Vince, I'm pretty sure there's something wrong with your dog's appetite." I nudged him with my elbow. "You told me Bud once ate an entire extension cord."

"And a wooden chair leg," Vince said, with a solemn nod. "And the lower third of a bathroom door."

"Good grief—are you sure he's not a goat?" my dad asked, gathering up the empty plates around him while looking moderately horrified. No doubt over the of repair costs he'd just tallied in his head. "See, this is why I don't like dogs."

"No, you don't like dogs because you're a mailman and they're one of your on-the-job hazards," Mom said, chuckling as she took the plates from him and headed off into the kitchen.

"Neither rain, nor sleet, nor bite of tiny yapping dog…" I recited a modified version of the Postal Worker's motto, mostly under my breath.

"You like *our* dog," Joelle pointed out as she grabbed her empty cereal bowl and excused herself from the table. "I saw you out the window yesterday, playing tag with her around the woodpile when you thought nobody was looking."

Dad grumbled something unintelligible-yet-dismissive.

I smirked, gauging Vince's reaction to the familial banter out of the corner of my eye. I was glad to have someone other than me offering assurance that my dad had a softer side. With how well things were going so far, I didn't think Vince had much to worry about when it came to finding a welcome place in my family one day.

"Hey Ang, you might want to show Vincent to where he'll be staying before it gets much later." Dad announced, getting to his feet. "I turned the electricity on to the playhouse and left a flashlight by the door."

Tyler scooted his chair back and gave Vince a discreetly sympathetic look.

"Uh…thanks?" In the time it took me to realize what Dad meant, he was already heading back down the steps to the basement. I called out after him, "I kind of hoped you were joking about keeping him out there!"

"Nope," Dad answered without looking back.

Okay, so maybe Vince had a few things to worry about.

~ ~ ~ ~ ~ ~ ~

Shortly after dinner, I walked Vince across the back yard and a hundred feet into the woods where the "playhouse" sat. The structure stood two stories high with wood siding that made it blend into its surroundings, each floor just ten by ten feet. My father had built it out of salvage scraps of choice lumber when we were small, bringing to life the dream fort he'd always wanted in his own childhood. I was only now starting to realize how little we'd appreciated the gesture.

Growing up, some of our friends had tree houses or converted deer stands to play in. We had a miniature furnished cabin. The playhouse was carpeted upstairs and down, with twin bunks on the ground floor and stairs wrapping around to a tiny deck up top. My dad ran a power line from the main house, allowing for lights and a fan upstairs, as well as a television. Our favorite part, though, was the trapdoor that let us drop from the upstairs to the top bunk below without having to go outside. Its only real drawback was the lack of a bathroom.

Oh, and no heat. Vince was particularly worried about that part. The sun was down and it was already a bit brisk, even by Minnesota standards.

I teased Vince about his lack of natural insulation and promised there were enough sleeping bags to keep him comfortable. We settled down in the upstairs of the playhouse and watched a movie—something about firefighters and time travel. Vince seemed more interested in kissing until our lips were chapped. I was happy to oblige him.

I fell asleep at some point before the movie ended, and he let me.

I hadn't slept well in the last two months. After what my former friend, Scott, tried to do while I was sleeping, I'd been plagued by vivid nightmares and the waking paranoia of someone coming into my bedroom. Vince was the only one who knew how poorly I was coping. Some guys might have been insulted that their lip-lock prowess wasn't enough to keep me conscious. Vince knew how big of a compliment it was that I trusted him so completely—found his nearness so comforting—I was able to slip away into the rest I'd been missing.

However, not even having him with me was enough to keep the darkness at bay. The dreams were often indistinct, yet the sensations were always the same.

Heavy breathing…crushing weight…a dim sense of panic.

Frenzied breath grazing my skin—friction heating my body.

I struggled and I ached.

I was drowning in tar—I couldn't breathe.

Hands grabbing…groping…ripping clothing.

*Get off, get off, GET OFF!*

I thrashed my way awake, mind spinning with confusion. For the first few seconds I didn't know where I was. I could have been standing on my head and I wouldn't have realized it. I only knew it was dark and I was being restrained, held down. I had to get away.

"Angel."

One whispered word, and my muscles relaxed. My mind calmed enough to piece coherent thoughts together. It wasn't completely dark—I could make out the blank TV screen sitting on its short stand near my feet. I was lying curled on my side, and the warm body wrapped around me from behind was Vince's. He'd molded himself against me, caged my flailing arms.

I was crying. Hot tears poured in steady rivulets down my cheeks.

"It's okay, babe. You're okay," Vince murmured into my ear.

A moment after I relaxed, his hold on me slackened. I was suddenly torn between relief and a bereft neediness I didn't understand. I couldn't remember ever wanting to be held so badly, not even as a child. I twisted around to grab for him, catching a handful of his shirt and writhing until I'd buried my face against his chest. He pulled me tight to him, petting my hair and my back, repeating soothing words I couldn't make out over my own sobs.

Swells of squeezing pain gripped my chest, alternating with roiling anger and the creeping chill of shame. They swept me along like the currents of a swollen, bankless river. For a few endless moments, I thought they meant to drag me under.

Then, it began to let up.

The uncontrollable pull eased by small increments, giving back tiny bits of my awareness. Vince was still there, talking to me—still holding me like I might fall if he let go. What he didn't know was that I'd already fallen. And he was my safety net.

As I regained control, I lifted a hand until I found the smooth curve of his jaw. "Did I...hit you?"

"Nah..." He answered, but his voiced pitched with omission. I mopped my face with my other hand and eased back enough to make out his concerned expression in the dim glow of the television. Nothing bleeding—that was good, at least. His lips pulled back in the start of a sheepish smile. "Okay, so you might have clipped my nose a little."

I slid my hand across his cheek and traced my fingers along the thin length of his nose. "Sorry," I whispered.

"Don't be." Vince caught the back of my hand and dragged it down, pressing his lips into my palm. "Just tell me how to make it better."

That was it, wasn't it? Something in me wasn't well. I needed it to get better—to stop it from bleeding into my thoughts and dreams.

*Please, God, please...make it go away.*

My eyes stung and watered. I pinched the bridge of my nose, trying to stop the threatening return of waterworks. "I don't know. I thought you being here..." I shook my head and shoved aside my own faulty reasoning. "I guess it just takes time."

Time and support. Those were consistently mentioned in the handful of articles on sexual assault I'd forced myself to read over the last few weeks. Somewhat less consistently were things like "counseling," and "therapy"…or the even less appealing, "medication."

"How much…time?" Vince asked, hesitating all the way through the question.

Dread cleaved its way into my heart, sharp and heavy. He was going to get tired of waiting. I'd put him through so much already, I knew that. It only made sense that I'd eventually exceed what he was willing to put up with. I managed to hold back any sound, but my tears flowed freely again. Not trusting myself to speak, I just shook my head.

"Hey, hey…no," he stammered, taking my face in his hands and wiping at my tears with his thumbs. His brows pulled together in a look of pained distress. "That came out wrong. I just mean…" He swallowed hard, as if the right words were lodged in his throat. If his agonizing wasn't enough to calm me, the way his fingers played through my hair and down my arm would have sufficed. "Do you think it'll still be like this…after we get married? When we…you know…"

*Married?* The fact that he'd just used the word with expectation threw me so hard it took a moment to grasp what he was stumbling over.

"Have sex?" I volunteered before I thought to temper my bluntness. Funny how it was easier for me to say, and I hadn't had it yet.

Vince nodded. "Am I going to be able to…touch you — show you how I feel like I want to? I mean, without you feeling like I'm trying to hurt you. Will you even *want* me to touch you?"

My heart went buoyant, and I chided myself for losing faith in his character so easily. He wasn't repulsed by my defectiveness, he was worried. And in the most tender way possible.

I lifted my hand again and traced the deep crease between his brows, trying to smooth it away. "I can't imagine not wanting you to touch me," I said, letting my sincerity sink into every word. "But...I don't know how I'll be then. Better, I hope. I just can't guess how long it'll take me to get used to being with you that way."

Vince's face gradually eased back to his more usual, unruffled state. The intensity in his gaze remained. "I'll just have to be careful," he reasoned, almost as though he were talking to himself as much as me. He brushed the backs of his fingers along the hollow of my cheek, then under my chin to lift it. "You tell me if I'm ever not being careful enough. Okay?"

I smiled, eyes welling with tears again. "I will."

His mouth curved into the half-smile I knew as a precursor to humor. "I might have to get fitted for body armor before the honeymoon, but I'm okay with that."

I laughed and gave his shoulder a swat. If he was trying to keep me from crying again, it was working.

His drollness faded back to sobriety as fast as it had surfaced. "We'll figure it out, babe." He gathered me in his arms and pressed his lips to my forehead, lingering a long moment. "Between you, me, and God...we'll figure it out."

My insides wound tight with gratefulness and longing. I shifted closer still, overcome with the desire to thank him for understanding. For loving me so well.

My lips found his without effort, without need for conscious thought. His kiss answered mine, gentle and tentative. His control was admirable.

Mine was not.

I wound my arms around Vince and lost myself in a pressing urgency. My mind seemed to break itself into separate pieces, all of them submerged beneath an unchecked surge of emotions. This was what I needed—more of him, more of us. The parts of my brain committed to chastity were shoved aside by the part that wanted nothing more than to make him happy.

Before I knew it, he'd rolled onto his back and taken me with him. As my weight settled against his chest, his lips trailed to my jaw. A thrill shivered through me. When I tried to mirror him, he stopped me, tucking my head under his chin.

Afraid I'd pushed him past the point of temptation, I went still. My whole focus centered on his rapid, shallow breaths and the pounding of his heartbeat beneath me. "I'm sorry," I whispered. As my sense of reason fully returned, another thought occurred to me. "Am I...crushing you?"

Vince laughed, the sound vibrating through his chest and into mine. "No."

I felt his lips nuzzling into my hair. "I...have to tell you something. You deserve to know."

The quiet tension in his voice piqued my concern. I braced my arms against the floor on either side of his chest and raised my head to look at him. Even in the dimness, the trepidation on his face was clear. "What's wrong?" My mind was already filing through an array of horrible theories. Whatever it was, I wanted it out in the open as soon as possible. "Tell me."

"I think..." He scanned my face and turned his head aside as he breathed out, "I think I might be a nymphomaniac. Or something…"

Of all the things I might have been preparing myself for, that wasn't one of them.

I froze and blinked down at him. "Um..." I had just enough presence of mind to extricate myself, shifting my weight off of him. I picked the side he'd turned his face toward, forcing him to look at me as I settled on my side. "You think...you're obsessed with sex?"

Vince nodded once, jaw muscles flexing. His hands fell away when I'd moved and now rested crossed at his chest.

Bemused, and not wanting him to feel any more ashamed than he obviously did already, I propped myself up on one elbow and covered his hands with mine. "You mean...you're addicted to porn? Or...are you trying to explain something else?"

He left one hand behind and drew the other one up to rub across his face in a motion I guessed was some attempt at concealing embarrassment. "No, not porn. Not exactly."

My guts felt as though they'd turned to warm gelatin. "What, then?" I gave his hand a pleading squeeze. "Please, tell me." Whatever it was, we could deal with it...

Couldn't we?

His fingers splayed across his face and he stared at me between his fingers for a moment before dragging his hand away. "I just....think about it all the time. All day, every day—I can't get it out of my head." He made a short sound like a laugh, but more aggravated. "If I weren't so afraid of screwing up my computer with a virus, I guess the porn thing would be an issue, too."

My distress began to ebb. *Nothing illegal or even particularly unexpected so far*, I reasoned. But why did he seem so upset about it? I tightened my hold on the back of his hand, trying to call back his full focus.

"I don't think that's being a nymphomaniac. I think that's just...biology. You're a guy," I said, with deliberate care. It seemed important he know I wasn't surprised or repulsed. "It's my understanding most guys think about sex a lot." I gave him my most reassuring smile, but a realization leaked sadness into it. "And you know what you're missing. That has to make it more difficult for you....remembering your ex-girlfriend and all."

Speaking my own worry aloud gave it new life, sending a wave of envy and sorrow crashing down on me. I wasn't at all shocked he'd still be preoccupied with memories. I couldn't compete—no, I *wouldn't* compete with that. Not yet. As easily as I seemed to lose my head with him, the thing that made me most sure of Vince's true character was that fact that he'd promised to respect my pre-marital boundaries. Despite the fact that such boundaries were foreign to his particular upbringing.

"No," Vince said, fixing me with a fierce look. "She's not the one I think about." He reached out and pressed a cool palm to my cheek, his thumb smoothing back to trace over my lips. "You don't get it. You don't know how bad I wanted you, even that first day we met in person. And the first time I kissed you...really kissed you..."

My lips tingled, in part from his touch and in part from the recollection he'd conjured. I leaned into his hand, only to be left adrift when he pulled away and turned his face toward the ceiling.

"I'm no better than Scott." The self-loathing in his expression matched his tone.

His declaration sent me reeling into bewilderment. "What are you talking about?" I wanted to shake him until he made sense. "You're nothing like him. You couldn't be more different."

"Angeli, listen to me." Vince looked my way again, something like disgust riding his voice. "You were so...innocent. Four days after I met you, I was ready to take everything you had to give. If you hadn't stopped me when you did—"

"No," I cupped my hand over his mouth to cut him off. "You listen to *me*." His brows lofted in surprise. Satisfied I had his undivided attention, I took my hand away and pressed it flat to the middle of his chest. "You *did* stop when I told you to. You would *never* try to force me."

He seemed to consider me for a drawn-out moment before his face slackened. "No," he whispered. "I wouldn't."

"So, stop beating yourself up." I bent closer, brushing my lips against his, nudging the tip of his nose with mine. I wanted to convey so much more, but it seemed cruel to risk tormenting him further. "It's not like my thought life is as pure as the driven snow," I added, pulling back to look at him while attempting a faint smirk. I felt it fall away with the return of worry over my increasingly lousy sense of self-control. "I seriously underestimated how difficult this was going to be."

Vince met my gaze with the most unfathomable look. He reached out then and pulled me to him in a grappling embrace. I let him, pillowing my head against his shoulder and nestling as close as I dared. "The only thing I want more than you, is to do right by you," he murmured into my ear.

"See…keep saying things like that, and it just raises the difficulty level," I warned on a teasing note.

"Difficulty level: Expert." I could hear the grin in his voice, and it made me laugh.

The tension between us had defused — for the time being, at least.

Gradually I became aware that the whole upstairs room of the playhouse was lightening with the first gray hint of dawn. It occurred to me then that I was technically supposed to be asleep, in my own bed. "I should head back down to the house. My dad goes to work early, and it'll be hard to sneak in once he's up." I processed my own words and cringed. "Ugh. I sound like some cliché rebellious teenager."

Vince tipped his head back and laughed. "Sneaking back into your bedroom after being out all night with your delinquent boyfriend?"

"Yeah, that's you." I smirked, mussing a hand through his carefully-groomed hair as I rose to my knees alongside him. "Such a bad-boy." Unable to resist, I dropped a kiss to his lips. "Good night."

As I pulled back to rise, Vince gave me a languid half-smile along with a correction, "Good morning."

# Ever After
-
# Part 3

"Mom, please let Vince sleep in the house." I got straight to the point as I walked into the upstairs living room where my mother sat on one end of the couch, strumming and tuning her acoustic guitar.

She glanced up, dark eyes assessing me with calm contemplation. She re-crossed her long legs and settled the instrument across her lap. "Does he not like staying in the playhouse?"

"He's not complaining, but he probably should," I said, letting genuine concern seep into my voice. "He was okay the first night, but it got a lot colder last night. I went up there this morning and found him buried under every blanket and beanbag chair we own. I have him thawing out in front of the stove, now." I jerked a thumb over my shoulder indicatively.

"I know we're in a bit of a cold snap, but I don't think it dropped below freezing." Mom frowned. "Then again, he is awfully thin. Nothing spare for insulation."

"Okay, yes, he's a little...horizontally challenged," I said, tamping down exasperation. "But he's also not used to this kind of climate."

"Ang, we never said he couldn't sleep in the house." Mom gave me a patient, thin-lipped smile. "He's welcome to the couch, just as long as he doesn't migrate anywhere else during the night."

"He...is?" I stared at her for a surprised beat. "But dad made it pretty clear where he wanted him to stay."

Mom plucked a few strings and shook her head. "Your father thought he might enjoy the cabin experience, that's all." She offered a knowing smile. "Besides, he's the first boy our firstborn decided to bring home. I think we're allowed to give him a little bit of a hard time."

I blew out a long breath, relieved I wouldn't have to argue the point. "Okay, well...thanks. I'll let him know." I leaned back into the door frame and stared down at my toes for a moment, suddenly feeling much younger and in need of affirmation. "So, I know it's only been a day and a half, but what do you think of him?"

My mom didn't answer right away. Instead she took her time setting her guitar aside on its stand and settled back, seeming to get comfortable.

Ever since I'd hit puberty, I was constantly told how much I favored my mother. Yet, I still couldn't see myself when I looked at her. We did share high cheekbones and darker pigment, but Mom's features — along with her mannerisms — were sharper and more refined. To me, my mother represented a sort of wizened femininity I wasn't sure I had much hope of attaining.

More than anything I wished I'd inherited her musical aptitude, but that particular artistic bent had gone to my sister. Along with the genteel temperament I also seemed to lack.

"I think," she began, "Vince is a very nice, intelligent young man."

Now there was a "mom" answer if ever I'd heard one.

Sensing she was holding back, I prompted, "But?"

"No 'but,'" Mom said, patting the cushion beside her in invitation. "I'm impressed he came all the way up here to see you. I can see why you're fond of him."

*Fond* didn't describe the half of it, but I wasn't about to go all gushingly-emotive-teenager on her. I moved closer to the couch and eased down to sit on the far arm. I wanted to hear whatever else she had to say, yet, at the same time, I was afraid to.

"You love him," she said. It was a statement, not a question.

I nodded, bracing myself for whatever warning she might issue. We'd already had every kind of "talk" imaginable, starting from the time I was around eleven years old. She'd decided I was mature enough for emotional, spiritual — and thanks to her nursing career, often medicinal — honesty. I'd long known what she expected *from* me and what she hoped *for* me.

Rather than reiterate an old point, she said, "He has a lot of potential. I think you're seeing him not just for what he is, but for what he could become."

I chewed on that for a moment before nodding. Her evaluation rang true. I didn't just see goodness in Vince, I saw greatness. Whatever it was he was supposed to grow into or achieve, I wanted to be there to help him through it. "I believe in him."

Mom looked first satisfied, then pensive. "And if he doesn't happen to live up to all of that potential...do you think you can still believe in him? Still respect him?"

Her unexpected inquiry warranted a stretch of silent consideration on my part. It was a valid question. More than that, it suggested my mother was taking me as seriously as I needed her to. I took heart in that unspoken vote of confidence as I formulated my response.

"If he never amounts to more than a volunteer firefighter and underpaid secretary, I'll still have all the respect for him I do now," I said, slow and certain. "And that's a lot. I know who he is — and that doesn't have anything to do with his education or job title or how much money he makes." I smiled confidently then, because I couldn't help it. "But I know he's going to be awesome. You'll see."

Mom gave me a hard-to-read look, and I held my breath. "Well, one of you is going to have to move eventually," she said, factual. "Have you decided who?"

With vague surprise, I resumed breathing and shook my head. "I don't know yet. I wanted to see what he thought of it up here before we hash that part out."

Mom nodded, forming a humored smile. "Let me know if I need to keep an eye out for winter clothes in his size. He'll probably need a full snowsuit if we're going to keep him alive."

"Uh...okay."

No one had wanted me to go on my crazy summer road trip less than my mother. And her disapproval had nearly stopped me. Whether she realized it or not, Mom was the only force outside of God who could possibly sway my determination to be with Vince. Yet instead, she sounded almost...accepting.

*Weirdness.*

I considered probing her for hidden skepticism, but the beckoning whistle of the teakettle reached me from the kitchen. I took it as a sign and jumped up. "That's mine."

It was probably best to exit the conversation while I was ahead.

I found Vince right where I'd left him—sitting cross-legged in front of the stove downstairs, draped in a thick blanket and flanked on one side by my adoring dog. The basement was dim, the firelight setting off his hair and stubble with an orange glow. I sank down at his free side and handed off one of the two mugs I'd brought along. "Here, this'll help."

Vince left one hand on Haley's head and used the other to extend half of the blanket over my shoulders. "What is it?" He peered at the dark contents of the mug with uncertainty.

"Hot tea with honey," I said, pressing my shoulder to his. "Black tea — nothing fancy."

"So...like sweet tea, but hot?"

I laughed. "Pretty much." It struck me as ridiculous that hot tea was almost as foreign a concept to him as sweet tea had once been for me. "Don't worry, I don't plan on introducing you to lutefisk or anything too culturally exotic."

"Lutefisk?" he asked, clearly unfamiliar with the term.

"It's a Scandinavian thing. Whitefish pickled in lye, dried, and then reconstituted into something that looks like a jellyfish and tastes like regret." I didn't actually know what regret tasted like — but I imagined if it did have a flavor, it would be lutefisk.

Vince's face contorted with disgust. "Why would anybody want to eat pickled fish?"

I shrugged. "Why would anybody want to eat pickled pig's feet?" I countered, remembering the jars of floating hooves I'd spotted at many a gas station during my stint south of the Mason-Dixon line.

"Good point." Vince smirked, testing a sip of his drink.

I spent a few moments content with Vince's nearness and half entranced with watching the fire flicker behind the glass door of the stove. "Good news. You get to sleep inside from now on."

"Thank God," Vince muttered. "I didn't want to alarm anybody, but I saw glowing eyes out on the deck last night. And I'm pretty sure I forgot to pack my vampire-slaying kit."

"Raccoons," I said, laughing. "Or maybe just a possum. They're pretty nosey."

"I like my story better." Vince cast me a puckish sidelong smile. "So, your brother and sister are okay with me, and I'm at least making progress with your parents. What all do you have planned for the rest of the week…and who else's good side do I need to get on?"

"Aikido is Tuesday night. You can just watch, if you'd rather not get thrown around," I began, noting his uncertain expression. He hadn't seemed to think much of my martial art club since he'd found out how often I came home from it with bruises. "You'll get to meet some of my friends eventually — maybe Wednesday night for bowling. They're mostly just curious about you." I cupped my mug, letting it heat my palms as I thought. "And then there's Guy at church. You'll meet him in a couple of hours when we go to the late service. He won't like you…but don't take it personally. He's just protective of me."

Vince quirked a brow in inquiry. "Some guy at your church?"

"No, his *name* is Guy." I chuckled. "He's kind of like my adopted grandfather. Even when I was a holy terror back in grade school, he was one of the only adults who treated me like he thought I was going to turn out okay." I smiled at the thought of the kind, blustering old man. "He once told me he didn't think any man could ever be good enough for me. Bless his delusional heart."

"In that case, I'll go ahead and consider it an honor to be judged unfit by him." Vince offered a lopsided grin.

"You should." I smiled. "Aside from that, the worst you'll have to put up with is following me to my classes this week. I got permission for you to shadow me to every class except for Life Drawing—I'll probably just drop you off at the mall or something while I'm taking that one."

"They won't let me sit in on your art class?" Vince gave me a perplexed look.

I looked down, swirling the contents of my mug as though I suddenly found it fascinating. "Not this one. It wouldn't really be respectful of the models if they let just anybody sit in."

Vince half-choked on a sip of tea. "Wait, you're drawing nude models?"

"Yeah," I said, trying to sound as nonchalant as possible. The truth was, I was still getting used to the idea myself. "You've had to take a lot of art classes for your graphic design degree. I figured you would have already had Life Drawing."

"I did," he said, surprise straining his voice a half-octave higher than usual. "But it sucked. All we drew was fruit, and the instructor didn't care about anybody showing improvement."

"Oh, sorry." I frowned in vague discomfort, venturing a glance his way. "I haven't drawn any fruit. Just…kinda skipped straight to anatomy."

"Naked people," Vince repeated.

"Yep."

Vince pulled his brows together, leaving a pause between us before finally asking, "Female models?"

I shrugged, trying to discern what he was getting at. "It's about half and half. Even had both at the same time once." Deciding I could have phrased that better, I added, "Nothing racy—just artistic contrast."

Vince's expression remained tight with thought, his jaw working side to side. "So...how many guys have you seen naked?" His tone was joking, but still betrayed a hint of insecurity.

I tilted my head back and laughed. "I don't know. I wasn't keeping track." I got a handle on my amusement and tried to level a more serious gaze on him. It helped that he still looked conflicted. "If I count Mom's medical textbooks, probably hundreds. And I think they *should* count, because that's pretty much the same way I see artistic nudity. I'm not planning on taking notes or making comparisons."

"Just wondering." Vince rolled his shoulders and shifted his attention to petting my dog. It took me a moment to realize he was probably embarrassed.

"It's not a big deal, trust me." I reached aside and laid my hand on his knee. "If I happen to go into the medical field one day, I'm probably going to end up dealing with a lot of live nudity. At least this way I'll have practice at being indifferent to it." I paused for a beat before hastily including, "In a professional context, I mean. Not...*completely* indifferent."

Now I was the one embarrassed.

A sly smile tugged at Vince's lips. "I hope not." He fixed me with a significant stare, and I could have sworn the radiant temperature of the stove spiked a hundred degrees.

"Anyway, I haven't quite worked up the nerve to put detail into anybody's bits and pieces. Especially the guys," I said, rambling out the admission. "The last time we had a male model, they made him sit in an old wooden chair in the middle of the room. By the time the class was over I had a halfway decent sketch of just the chair."

Vince now looked thoroughly amused. "Your professor didn't notice?"

"I told her I was focusing on shadows and negative space."

"Nice save." Vince laughed.

Just as he looked ready to poke fun at my discomfort, guitar music came drifting down the stairwell. Vince identified it a half second before I did and gaped at me in some combination of horror and fascination. "Is that....Dueling Banjos?"

"Sounds like it." I winced outright. My mother had to be deliberately near the upstairs landing in order to project the iconic tune.

"She's taunting me, isn't she?"

I patted his knee in consolation and apology. "Try to take it as a good sign. She only teases the people she likes."

Vince's skeptical frown twisted into a cautious smirk. "Well then, here's to your mom liking me," he said, lofting his tea mug my way. "And here's to me, hoping she doesn't pick Sweet Home Alabama as an encore."

I tapped my mug against his with a *clink* and leaned into his side, stifling a giggle I didn't know I had in me. "I'll drink to that."

~ ~ ~ ~ ~ ~ ~

"Pretend you like each other!"

Joelle's tone was playful as she scuttled a few steps to one side and snapped yet another photo. It was a cool but cloudless Tuesday afternoon, and she had been taking advantage of the fact by herding me and Vince all around the woodsy side-lawn of my parent's house for couple's pictures. Our backdrops included the wood pile, the rope swing, random boulders, and now lastly, a wall of old railroad ties my father had used in his efforts at cost-free landscaping.

Vince wore a navy button-up, and I'd had enough forethought to put on a fitted hunter-green sweater — another of the few flattering things in my closet. My one bit of rebellion against fashion sense was my insistence on going barefoot. With the weather turning, it was one of my last chances to feel grass between my toes before the lawn was buried under snow for four to five months.

The whole photo thing felt silly to me, but the play of charisma between Vince and my sister kept me genuinely smiling through most of the session. It was a good thing too — as the best I could manage on command was a forced show of teeth that undoubtedly resembled more of a grimace. My sister compensated for this by catching me off guard with cheeky remarks and vocal impressions of a video game character she knew I found unbearably cute.

"Good, good," Joelle called out after convincing me to kiss Vince's cheek. She flipped her honey-brown hair back over her shoulders and gestured with competent directness. "Now, give her a kiss. You know you want to."

"Almost as much as I want to keep breathing." Vince waggled his copper brows at me in an over-the-top look of allure. His gaze flickered to my lips, then back to my eyes. "I think she's trying to get me in trouble with your dad," he whispered at a volume that ensured my sister would hear.

"Photographer/client confidentiality." Joelle waved her hand in a lithe gesture of dismissal. "If he finds out, it won't be from me." She then began singing the chorus to *Kiss the Girl*, from The Little Mermaid movie.

Sufficiently humored and goaded, I initiated the kiss and Vince met me halfway. It wasn't just for show. For a moment, I suspect we both forgot my sister was there. The contact between us was soft and sweet, lingering to the point where Vince finally turned his face away with a look of mild abashment.

I laughed.

Joelle made an airy, triumphant sound and lowered her camera. "Well, I'm sure I got at least a few decent ones. I'll let you two know when they're ready to be seen." She flashed a pleased smile, tilting her head aside as she regarded us with a curious look. "Cute couple," she said with a sigh, then spun on her toes and departed.

"Thanks, sis!" I called after her, watching as she flounced around the side of the house and bounded weightless up the steps of the back deck like a woodland elf.

My sister had the figure of a gymnast, the face of a model, and the voice of an angel. An effervescent whirlwind of sound, motion, and zeal—Joelle was, in many ways, my antithesis. She was luminous, while I tended toward brooding. She enjoyed people, I enjoyed fictional characters. She inspired, I intimidated. She sashayed, I lumbered.

And for one penetratingly insecure moment, I wondered if Vince was with the wrong sister.

"She's a trip," Vince said, chuckling. When I glanced back I found him studying me with an intensity that quelled my self-doubt. He stood and offered both of his hands to help me up.

"A trip to Disney Land, maybe." I laughed, finding some genuine admiration in my voice as I accepted his assistance. "She sings, she dances, she acts... she takes pictures. Never a dull moment with Joelle around."

Vince kept a hold on my left hand as he walked us toward the tree line. "Sounds like you'll have a few more pictures for your album." Something in his tone told me he wanted to talk about something, and he apparently wanted to be moving at the same time. Given I'd shown him all of the pictures from my summer road trip just before Joelle's photo session, I could guess at what was on his mind.

Vince's mood had darkened substantially when he came across a picture of me and Scott standing together at the top of the Empire State Building. I'd nearly forgotten about it. I had briefly considered burning the last reminder of my host from the New York portion of the road trip, but it happened to be the only evidence that I'd stood on the 86th floor of what was once the tallest building in the world. My own sense of catharsis seemed to pale next to the conviction that I ought to keep an accurate record of my adventure. But I wasn't sure Vince had fully accepted my explanation.

"I think I should start a new photo album," I said, keeping so close in step that our shoulders brushed. He steered us in a slow circuit around the perimeter of my parent's few acres of property. Here the grass blended with moss, soft as suede and cool against my bare feet. "Since I'm kind of starting a new story, maybe it's time to close volume one and move on to volume two."

Vince gripped my hand tighter, casting me a sidelong look of assessment. "I need to ask you something about volume one." Caution tinged his voice. "But I don't want you to get offended or take it wrong."

"Thanks for the warning." I mustered a reassuring smile, while bracing myself internally. I wasn't sure what he could want to know that I hadn't already told him in one of our nightly phone conversations. "Ask anything you want."

He seemed to hesitate, scanning the ground ahead of our steps. "Has Scott tried to contact you since...?" Vince trailed off, his expression betraying tense concern. It was a reasonable question, but from his tone I realized he was afraid I might take it as accusing.

"Just once, before I blocked his email and instant messenger access," I said, focusing on the anger the incident raised in me. Anger was better than the hurt and guilt that thoughts of Scott usually invoked. "And it started out indirect. He...included me on some email newsletter list he'd sent out to all of his friends and family when he started college. I don't know why I read it. He was mostly whining about his dorm room and the cafeteria food—rambling about his classes. But then he included a list of the girls he thought were attractive enough to be worth his attention, and it felt like...I don't know. Like he included me on the email list just so he could rub that part in my face."

"Maybe he thought he could make you jealous." Vince's flinty expression matched his tone, controlled anger giving his face the look of a predatory bird.

I clenched my teeth so my words came out strained between them, "All it made me want to do was contact those girls and warn them not to fall asleep if he happens to be anywhere nearby."

My own bitterness felt like stomach acid at the back of my tongue. Then again, that might be exactly what it was. Even my blood burned caustic through my veins when I thought of Scott taking advantage of some other girl who might be as naive as I was to trust him. Some other girl, who might not be physically able to fight him. Some other girl…who might believe him when he blamed her.

Vince squeezed my hand, bringing me back to myself and quenching some of the mordant ache in my chest. "Did you tell him that?"

I shook my head and looked down. "I should have. First, I just sent him a message telling him to take me off his mailing list. I told him the truth—that he'd hurt me badly, and I wasn't ready to hear anything from him. That I might never be ready." I paused to gauge Vince's reaction, but he seemed to balance himself between seething and listening. I went on, "He shot back this short, angry email—something to the effect of: if I actually believed in my "stupid religion," then I *had* to forgive him."

Vince's tone plummeted with disgust. "That son of a *$%&#!"

*You have no idea*, I thought, shaking off the unpleasant recollection of Scott's mother.

"I guess it finally hit me then that he wasn't sorry," I said, embarrassed it had taken such a backhanding for me to recognize the obvious.

"Oh, he's sorry, alright," Vince uttered with dangerous calm. "Sorry excuse for a human being."

I stopped walking and ran my free hand down Vince's rigid arm. He reminded me of a bowstring. Slim, strong, and taut. Righteous indignation flared cold in his eyes, making him look much older than I'd ever seen. For a passing moment, I thought there must be nothing quite so fierce as the wrath of an otherwise gentle man.

"Stop that," I said, lightly.

Vince startled at my request, his gaze refocusing on me rather than whatever was going on in the depths of his mind. "Stop what?"

"Stop plotting his slow, torturous demise." I reached out and pressed my free hand flat to the center of Vince's chest, feeling his heart pound hard and fast under my palm. "I've already done that. Trust me—it's not healthy."

I felt Vince's grip on my hand slacken as disconcerted frustration creased his brow. "You think you have to forgive him, don't you."

"Eventually," I said, with no shortage of reluctance. I added quickly, "But for *me*, not for him. It doesn't mean I have to forget, or pretend it was no big deal...or let anything go back to the way it was." I paused. "Hating him is just too much dead weight for me to keep dragging around. It's useless, it's...consuming." I stared hard into Vince's conflicted eyes and pressed a little more weight into my palm in emphasis. "And I have better things to be consumed by."

Vince's tense look faded into something vastly more significant. He renewed his grip on my hand and lifted it, pressing his lips to each of my knuckles.

A shiver ran through the center of me and I looked away, suddenly conscious that we stood in plain sight of the house. But I didn't resist when he pulled me into a tight embrace. I set my chin on his shoulder and closed my eyes, reveling in the security I hadn't known I needed.

We stood like that for a long while, Vince's fingers playing through my hair and down my back. "I have another question," he said, making no move to release me.

I opened my eyes, brushing my chin over his shoulder as I turned to look at his face. He didn't look at me, however. His pensive gaze stayed locked and unfocused. He was either about to present another serious topic, or crack a joke to lighten the mood. I couldn't begin to guess which. In truth, it was one of the traits about him I found so captivating. "What is it?" I laid my temple against his shoulder and waited.

He didn't respond right away. When he did it was in a quiet, unsteady voice. "If I were to possibly...one day...ask you to marry me—" he glanced at me and then away, as if afraid he'd lose his train of thought. "Do you think you might say 'yes'?"

My heart went buoyant, catching somewhere low in my throat. *I think he just proposed a proposal.*

Did that make it a pre-proposal? Was there even such a thing? Not that it mattered, really...

Vince was waiting for my answer, nervous vulnerability pulling his brows up and together. I didn't have to point out that I wouldn't have let things get this far if I didn't think we could handle permanency. He wasn't looking for a sober list of the obstacles we still faced, or why I thought those obstacles were worth facing. He only needed the reassurance that we were both on the same page of the same story.

I was more than happy to give him that bookmark.

"Possibly, one day," I smiled with every bit of sincerity in me. "Yes."

# Ever After
## -
## Part 4

After successfully dragging Vincent around with me to classes all day for the first half of the week, I decided it was time to introduce him to a few of my ragtag friends. Starting with my best friend, Elsie.

Out of all of my real-life acquaintances, Elsie was the one most likely to understand the online connection Vince and I had originally shared. In part because she was even more of an unmitigated geek than I was. And in part because she'd been the one who found and brought me into the story-writing community we now all had in common. Vince had a knack for creating genius villain characters, I had a fondness for coming up with warriors, and Elsie favored the slightly deranged inventor archetypes.

In theory, we should all get along just fine. But when it came to in-person socialization, Elsie could be quite the wild card. I had just enough sense to be worried.

While we waited on Elsie's arrival, Vince gave himself a tour of my bedroom. I wasn't looking forward to this part, but it was only fair. I'd already had my chance to examine his bedroom and decide what the space said about him.

"I haven't really updated in a while," I said, propping open my door as per house rules. "No laughing."

"Babe, I still live with my parents, and sleep on a bunk bed." Vince smirked as he walked in past me, glancing around at the tacky phosphorescent stars and planets dotting the pale blue walls.

My room was less than half the size of his — just enough room for a full-size bed in one corner, a mismatched dresser, and a too-small desk. My dad had built a shelf above the dresser to display the Star Trek and Babylon 5 action figures I refused to grow out of. A large wire cage sat along my dresser, housing my recently acquired set of young rats — one gray and one blonde.

Vince studied one of my wolf posters for a moment before noticing the full wall mural over my desk. "You did this?" he asked, sounding almost awed.

My heart expanded, as though he'd just paid me a great compliment. "When I was thirteen. I was a little bit obsessed at the time." The painting was one of the few things in my room I was proud of. It depicted an epic space battle between an exotic array of ships—all on the backdrop of a sun rising over some desolate alien planet. "Some girls had their heads in the clouds. My head was somewhere on the other side of the galaxy."

Vince gave me one of his contemplative half-smiles before shuffling over to the rat cage. "Priscilla and Nene'?"

I nodded, stepping up beside him. I reached in and scooped up the gray one, offering her out to him. "This one's Priss."

Vince accepted the sleek animal with no sign of hesitation, cupping her in one palm and holding her close against his chest as he rubbed a fingertip between her ears. His lack of squeamishness warmed me as much as his deliberate carefulness.

"So, you're not just good with dogs," I said, taking Nene' out next and setting the blonde rodent on my shoulder. Nene' hooked her tail loosely around the back of my neck and began the vigorous process of washing her face with her paws.

"I never really thought of these as pets until you started talking about them." Vince shrugged. "I don't see why people find their tails so creepy. They feel kind of...neat." He smoothed a finger along Priscilla's bare, scaly tail. His gaze shifted off to one side of me then, and he looked briefly spooked.

I turned, following his gaze in the general direction of my closet. Somehow I didn't think my affinity for men's clothes and camouflage patterns was enough to give him the shock he'd just tried to downplay. After a second I spotted the likely culprit grinning down at us from the top shelf. "Oh, the clown," I said, crossing the room to close the accordion doors. "I forgot that was up there. I think my grandma gave it to me when I was five or six."

Vince gave the closed closet a wary stare. "Is it the kind that moves when you wind it up?"

"And plays music."

"Yeah…" he said, with a hint of a shudder. "You don't happen to have a padlock for that door, do you?"

I tried not to laugh. Vince had repeatedly mentioned an extreme distrust for clowns, but I'd taken it as him being humorous. His candid reaction now made me think this 'distrust' might border on phobia.

*Okay, so he has a problem with clowns, but not rodents. At least he has his priorities straight.*

I moved back to Vince and took Priscilla from him, placing both rats back into their cage. "If you're having a Stephen King moment, we can go wait upstairs. Elsie should be here —"

"Speak of the devil's dungeon master and she shall appear." Elsie's brash alto voice carried from the doorway. Elsie herself stood in full view, her willowy form draped in an oversized tie-dye T-shirt and adorned with a pair of 12-sided dice she'd converted into a set of dangling earrings. Her arms splayed out at her sides like she'd just finished a musical number and expected applause. Auburn hair fell about her shoulders in a wild mane to frame round, ethnically muddled features. "Sorry I'm late — my mom made me re-clean my room before I could leave. If you ask me, the ol' hag's been in a bad mood ever since she discovered her first gray pube hair last week."

"Overshare!" I held up a hand to cut her off, too late.

Elsie's attention shifted. Her ice-gray eyes fixed on Vince and narrowed in challenge. "Nightfang."

Vince squared his shoulders. "Proxy."

"Okay, real names, please?" I interjected. "Prox...er...Elsie, this is Vincent. Vincent...Elsie." I shot my friend a warning look. At least she'd referred to him by the name of his neutral character rather than one of the outright villains. Thanks to several quirky years of experience, I wasn't *entirely* confident in her ability to distinguish fiction from reality.

Elsie gave me a dramatic eye-roll. "I'm just playing. Don't get your panties in a wad." She stepped into the room and stuck out a hand for Vince to shake. "Nice to finally make your acquaintance. I gotta say—I've enjoyed some of your work. Especially that big elaborate plotline you did with Excise last year."

Vince seemed to relax, accepting the handshake with an easy smile. "Thanks."

Elsie kept shaking his hand a little too long, smiling all the while. "And this is probably where I should let you know...if you hurt my best friend, I'll have to castrate you with a rusty cheese grater." She released his hand then, the demented cheerfulness in her voice reflected in her face.

"Fair enough," Vince nodded, looking unfazed.

"Fan-freaking-tastic." I sighed, rubbing a palm down my face in exasperation. Though I had to admit, some small piece of me was touched. I'd spent much of middle school and high school verbally—and sometimes physically—defending

Elsie from the abundance of kids who didn't know how to tolerate her eccentricities. Up until this point, I couldn't recall being on the receiving end of her concern. Never mind the fact that she wasn't capable of real violence beyond writing about it.

*It's the thought that counts.*

"So, what were we doing tonight?" Elsie asked, as though she hadn't just issued a warped threat. "Something about balls...?"

"Bowling," I said, interrupting her snicker. I could swear she had the mind of a twelve-year-old boy. "We're meeting Millune and Sheila at Spare Pinz."

"Right," Elsie nodded as though the plan met with her approval. "How about afterward we all meet back at my house? I came up with this hilarious new game. First, we sit out on the back porch and wait for the drunken college students to come stumbling into my back yard," she leaned toward Vince to add an aside, "Our house is in a low spot—gravity just kinda funnels them there." She looked back to me and returned to her enthusiastic proposal, "Then, we hit them with the garden hose and see how fast they can scale the fence."

"Sounds like a 911 call waiting to happen," Vince said, looking both amused and dubious.

"Hey, you try living in the middle of the bar-muda-triangle," Elsie raised her chin at him. "A girl has to fend off boredom somehow."

Vince didn't volunteer his rather extensive history of growing up in and around bars, so I decided not to bring it up. I hadn't told Elsie much about Vince's background—largely because she hadn't asked. I'd long ago accepted that she was allergic to ingesting and/or sharing much by way of personal information. I sometimes wondered if it was simply the price her hyper-creative mind demanded.

"Oh, check this out…" Elsie's countenance brightened as her attention jumped to something new. She reached into the back pocket of her jeans and pulled out a small sketch pad. "I reinvented one of my characters as a bad guy." She caught the edge of the pad with her thumb and flipped through it. Flashes of intensely detailed werewolves, robots, superheroes, and mutants all ran together in her unique comic-like style. She landed on a central page and waved the pad in Vince's face.

Vince's brows lifted as he took the offered pad and studied the drawing in question. "Is her hand a C-clamp?" he asked, turning the image sideways.

"Her other hand is a Gatling gun," Elsie said, proudly jabbing a finger toward one part of the image.

Thinking my boyfriend and best friend might actually be getting used to each other, I decided things were stable enough for us to go out in public. "I'm going to let the girls know when to meet up. You two play nice," I directed more than asked as I turned and stepped out.

It took me two minutes to call Sheila and work out a departure time. When I returned, I found Vince laying on my bed in a fetal position, wheezing. Elsie had her hands up and her back to the nearby wall, looking both guilty and defensive.

I went straight to Vince's side, bewildered and unsure over how concerned I should be. "What in the heck just—?"

"Not my fault!" Elsie said, her pale eyes wide. "Okay, like ninety-percent not my fault. We were just goofing around."

Vince caught his breath, still coiled around himself protectively. "She hit me."

"Who blocks with their crotch?!" Elsie's voice hit a shrill pitch and sped up. "He was making fun of my character's fighting style. I was just giving him a little demonstration—that's all. I didn't expect him to *move* like that."

I touched Vince's arm, worry for him warring with irritation for my impulsive friend. I bent close to Vince's ear. "Do you need an ice pack?"

"Not sure yet," he groaned, struggling to sit doubled over at the foot of my bed.

I rubbed a soothing hand down his back, unable to relate but feeling flinchingly sympathetic all the same. "Seriously, Elsie?" I shot my longtime friend one of the more livid glares in my arsenal.

"Look, it was an accident." Elsie held out her hands as if to ward off my potential wrath. "If it'll make it up to you, I'll let him punch me in the boob." She glanced down at her meager bosom, as if trying to decide something. "But go for the left one—it's already got a funny slant to it. You might even fix something."

Vince shook his head as he lifted it to glance between us. "No, thanks. I don't hit girls."

Elsie gave me a helpless shrug. "Well, there you go. It's not my fault your boyfriend is all sexist. I was totally willing to go tit-for-tat. Or I suppose more accurately it would be tit-for—"

"Hey Elsie, how about we just meet you at the bowling alley in an hour," I said, flattening my tone. "Okay?"

Elsie deflated like an unplugged bouncy castle. "Fine," she said, exhaling in a huff. "For the record...I'm sorry." She slumped her shoulders and headed for my door. Without looking back I caught her mutter not so under her breath, "But if I could break him on accident, I don't know how you figure he's going to survive you and all your butch glory."

That last remark sparked my annoyance to full-blown anger—enough so that I didn't regret suggesting Elsie leave. I sank down beside Vince so our sides touched and waited for him to recover. No sooner had I made contact with him than my agitation began to ebb, as if my turbulent emotions were lightning and he was a grounding wire.

*How does he do that?*

Gradually Vince sat up straighter and his breathing evened out. "Well," he spoke at last, his eyes tense with some blend of pain and irritation. "That could have gone better."

"I'm really sorry." I grazed a hand up and down his tense back. Elsie might have been crass, but she wasn't exactly wrong in her assessment. She'd known me long enough to recognize that, for a girl, I was aggressive at best and brutish at worst. But what she didn't know was that something about Vince changed me. Just being near him made me calmer...softer. Yet, at the same time, I'd never felt stronger.

"Are you going to be okay?" I asked. "Should I cancel bowling?"

Vince shook his head, jaw tight. "I'm alright."

"I don't *think* she did it on purpose. She's like me — about as graceful as a one-legged elephant." I paused a beat, adding, "And half as tactful."

"Any chance she might be getting back at me for one of my friends trying to strangle you?" he asked, somber.

I shook my head. "No, she doesn't even know about that." The memory from two months prior ran through my mind like a cut scene from a video game — vivid but still somewhat unreal.

At one point during my original road trip visit, one of Vince's overly competitive classmates had offered to "teach" me an Aikido move. When my flexibility thwarted his hold, the young man put me in a noose-like headlock and wrenched me off my feet — clamping my airway and coming perilously close to breaking my neck. I'd managed to get away from him before passing out. Vince came upon the scene almost too late, and ended up looking after me as I recovered.

The bizarre burst of violence wasn't my favorite recollection of all my adventures. But in the weeks since, I'd come to wonder if it hadn't been a tipping point in Vince's feelings for me. Would he have decided to pursue me clear across the country if that incident hadn't spurred so much protectiveness and worry in him? I wasn't sure, but if it *had* contributed to Vince's sense of persistence, I couldn't entirely regret that it happened.

Vince took a deep breath and his tension seemed to unfurl around him. "She's your best friend, and you didn't mention something like that to her?" I wasn't certain if he was still irked, or simply in more pain than he wanted to show.

"We don't usually talk much about...well...anything that matters," I said, knowing that must sound strange. Admitting it out loud caused a twinge of the same loneliness I'd dealt with for most of my high school experience. "She'll talk about games and comic books all day, but serious stuff makes her uncomfortable. She's a master at changing subjects and making it seem like it's just her ADD meds wearing off." I gave a disquieted shrug. "I feel bad for her sometimes. I'm afraid there might be some sort of awful, traumatic reason she likes to live in her own little world and won't let anybody get too close. But if there is...she won't tell me."

Vince gave me a long look. "Did you tell her what her cousin did to you?"

My guts knotted at the reminder I wasn't quite expecting. "I did—a couple of weeks ago. I had to, so she'd know why I couldn't stand hearing about him anymore." My fingers fidgeted in my lap as though they had erratic little minds of their own. "I was afraid she wouldn't believe me. Or...that she'd take Scott's side and not want to be friends anymore."

I blinked and Scott's face flashed against my eyelids; his chilling, carnal expression seared into some dark corner of my mind. I sucked in a sharp breath to steady myself.

Vince ran a hand down my arm and laced our fingers together, stilling the twitchy movements mine had been making. "How'd she take it?"

"She was surprised, but she believed me." I made myself look at Vince, memorizing his every distinct feature and freckle—determined to replace the bad that lingered in my head with the good right in front of me. "I know it upset her, at least. It was the first time I've seen her be serious about *anything* for more than ten seconds."

He seemed to relax by small increments, rubbing circles in the back of my hand with his thumb. "What do you think she's going to do with that knowledge?"

"I don't know." I shook my head in resignation. "What would you do if you found out one of your favorite cousins was an attempted rapist?" When he looked taken aback by the question I squeezed his hand. "That was rhetorical. What I'm saying is...it can't be easy for her to deal with, either. I'm just grateful she didn't doubt me. And she didn't try to justify or defend what he did."

Vince didn't appear entirely settled, but he at least seemed to reconcile something internally. He let a stretch of silence fall in punctuation before asking, "So, do I need to go buy a codpiece before I meet the rest of your friends?"

"As much as I'd like to see that...no." I laughed. "I don't think we have to worry about the rest of them."

Or at least, I *hoped* we didn't.

~ ~ ~ ~ ~ ~ ~

Spare Pinz was located at the edge of town in a sizable old cinderblock building. The sign out front was made up of vintage neon lights in rainbow colors, half of the letters perpetually burned out. The bowling alley had been there as long as I could remember, and I'd never once seen the sign fully lit.

After the near-sterilizing fiasco with Elsie, I was a bit on edge. I noticed a jostling, drunken trio of college guys as we walked past them on our way into the building. Their loud talking and guffawing overlapped so much I nearly missed it when one directed a crude proposition my way. I ignored him.

Vince didn't. He shot the group a look over his shoulder and slid an arm around the small of my back, hooking his thumb through the belt loop at my opposite hip.

*Well, that's a little more possessive than hand-holding.*

"Marking your territory?" I asked, trying to look vaguely annoyed on principle. The truth was, his sudden assertiveness had ignited a fuzzy warmth in my stomach.

"Just being clear." Vince cast me a wry half-smile, keeping tightly in step at my side. "In my experience, you have to be extra-obvious with drunk people if you want to avoid any *misunderstandings*."

"By 'misunderstandings,' do you mean bar fights?"

He gave a casual shrug, smile widening. "Semantics."

"I'm pretty sure I could take them if they got stupid enough to touch me," I said, popping my knuckles for effect. "Their balance has to suck right now."

Vince chuckled. "And I'm pretty sure I don't want to see you get arrested."

We were still more or less moving as one attached unit as he reached ahead and pulled open the glass doors. My friends had picked a lane within eyeshot of the entrance, beneath the glow of a tacky fiber-optic palm tree. Elsie hung back at the table while the other two approached us, shameless fascination written all over their expressions.

Sheila led the inquisition. Her straight, ash-blonde hair was pulled back into twin buns, accented with a paisley red handkerchief that clashed with her violet, horn-rimmed glasses. Despite the chilly weather she was dressed light — yoga capris and a clingy red tank top showing off her ever-pale skin. She was the smallest of all of us, but made up for her diminutive size with copious amounts of apathy and sarcasm. "So this is *the guy*," she said, inspecting Vince like a jeweler doing an appraisal. She tilted her head and tapped her chin in drawn-out thought. "He looks good on you."

"Yeah…thanks," I said, then motioned between her and Vince. "This is Sheila."

Millune sidled up just behind her, a reserved-yet-hopeful look on her deep bronze face. Her floor-length red dress swished around her ankles, its swirls of intricate gold threadwork matching her headscarf while complementing her necklace and many rings. This was special occasion attire, I realized at once. Supposing this was likely her way of honoring Vince's significance to me, I gave her a grateful smile as I introduced them. "And this is Millune, my former prom date." I referenced my humiliating senior prom experience to help Vince place her.

I was relieved to realize the entire incident seemed diminished in my own mind. Having all of my guy friends reject me, being mistaken for a lesbian, falling down the stairs at the grand march, becoming the butt of so many jokes for the last two months of high school—they almost felt like unfortunate things that happened to someone else.

Maybe one day I could feel that way about everything that had hurt me.

Vince shook Sheila's hand and then Millune's, without removing his arm from around me.

"Wow...you're even skinnier in person than your pictures!" Millune's Somali accent carried thick in her melodic voice. Considering the fact that her family had fled to the United States just five years earlier—landing her and her siblings in the public school system with almost no help transitioning—Millune's grasp of English was quite good. Her grasp on social and cultural expectations was another matter.

Vince took the frank observation in stride, patting his concave mid-section. "Well, they say the camera adds ten pounds. I might have actually needed those."

Sheila jabbed her elbow back to nudge Millune in a less-than-subtle reprimand, never taking her eyes off Vince. "Don't mind her—she's just jealous. As it so ironically happens, the only one of us who's never had a boyfriend before is currently the only one of us *with* a boyfriend."

Elsie called our attention her way then with a, "Hey guys, check it out..."

I'd thought she was hanging back out of some contrite effort to avoid embarrassing me further. I was sadly mistaken.

Elsie stepped away from the ball rack after selecting two bowling balls of a marbled azure color—both of which she now held together just below her beltline as she declared, "I'm blue-balling!"

*Dear Jesus, please make this night go by faster.*

I turned to bury my face in Vince's shoulder. He chuckled in my ear, uneasy.

"Super classy," Sheila called back. She tugged at my arm then, trying to peel me away from Vince and steer me toward their table. "Come on. This is going to be just like lunch hour back in high school...with a slightly higher threat of blunt force trauma."

"You really know how to sell an idea, Sheila," I said, letting her half-drag me. I realized then how literally she meant her claim when I glanced around and spotted at least three other alleys occupied by clusters of our former graduating class. Four months after graduation, and it seemed as though everyone was still in town.

Six guys from the lacrosse team were causing an oblivious-yet-jovial racket at the far end of the lanes. To our immediate left was half of the former student council, all chattering amiably amongst themselves. They were never a mean bunch, as I recalled — just cliquish. I waved to Vera, the petite red-headed girl I recalled being our school photographer. She gave me a blank stare before recognition seemed to dawn and she waved back. For a split second I considered trying to strike up a first time conversation with her, if only because I had nothing to lose by it, but she turned her full attention back to her friends before I could act.

Two lanes to the right I recognized more faces and my anxiety ratcheted up several notches. Flaxen-haired Mindy and her ever-vicious bestie, Sarah, were perched on the laps of two brawny-looking guys I didn't recognize — though, judging by their matured faces and mugs of beer, they were on the graduating end of college. Sarah caught me staring and her model-pretty, au latte face warped into a sneer. I looked away, hoping she didn't decide to renew her lease on tormenting me or my friends. I didn't want Vince to see me get arrested any more than he did.

Yes, this felt like high school. That excruciatingly uncomfortable phase I was more than ecstatic I'd left behind. Only, it wasn't far enough behind me. I had the sudden thought that as long as I was still in my hometown, this trapped feeling was going to keep cropping up—just like so many of my former classmates who hadn't managed to escape its vacuous pull.

"You okay, babe?" Vince's voice was low in my ear, snapping my focus off my own brooding. He hovered close behind me as a reassuring presence and warmth. I leaned back into him and he slid an arm around my shoulders and collarbone, anchoring my back to his chest.

"Yeah." I turned my head and gave him a grateful smile. "Ready to play?"

Vince grinned back at me. "I think I'm...*ready to roll.*"

"Puns are the lowest form of humor," Elsie chirped out from across the table, pausing in the middle of typing out a player name to look our way. Her lips curled into a manic smile and she raised her voice, "Oh, and as my friends I just want you all to know...you have permission to touch my balls." That earned her a round of exasperated sounds from everyone.

Elsie cackled.

Millune and Sheila were already on the overhead scoreboard as "Milly" and "She-Ra." Elsie added herself as Proxy, and Vince followed suit with Nightfang—which compelled me to use my favorite online moniker: Peril. This was shaping up to be oddball bowling at its finest.

Vince won the first game. Elsie came in last, with jester-worthy style and an exhausted repertoire of ball jokes. To my great relief, everyone seemed to be having a good time.

By then the crowds had thinned. Mindy, Sarah, and their dates disappeared without incident. I was just starting to unwind when Vince excused himself to go hunt for a restroom. No sooner had he started across the bowling alley than Millune and Sheila landed in the hard plastic chairs on either side of me.

*And now, for the unsolicited opinions…*

"We like him," Sheila said in a conspiring tone, peering at me over the top of her glasses. "He's funny and cute…in a nerdy sort of way. Not really what we would have pictured for you, but it could work—"

"He's too skinny," Millune interjected on the other side of me. Her plump lips were pursed and her black brows pulled together in a look of genuine concern. "You need to feed him more, so he doesn't get sick. My dad was too skinny before we came to America…"

Everything in me softened toward Millune, and I patted her arm in appreciation. Skinniness meant something entirely different to her than it did to most first-world natives. "You guys lived in a refugee camp, Mill. Vince is just…naturally lean."

Although he did seem to have trouble remembering to eat. I already nagged him enough about regular meals, but it wasn't because I was preoccupied with his weight. His overall health concerned me — physical, mental, emotional, and spiritual. I knew without hesitation the concern was mutual.

Sheila spoke up again with, "Personally, I'm disappointed he doesn't have a Southern accent."

I rolled my eyes at that. "At least he's got the manners," I said, watching as Elsie went through an ungainly dance routine before finally turning her back to the alley. She released the ball in a clunky two-handed roll that bounced once between her knees and meandered into the gutter. I golf-clapped for her, and she raised her middle finger in salute.

"Mmm...he does have good manners. They sure don't make guys like that around here," Sheila said, looking wistful. "Does he have any brothers?"

I smirked at her. "Only child. Sorry."

"He makes you happy." Millune spoke so quietly I almost didn't catch it. When I looked back her way, she wore a faint smile and her deeply dark eyes had misted over. "I never seen you smile so much." It was a simple observation, but put with a poignancy that cut straight to my heart. Before I could decide how to respond, Vince came sauntering back up to our table.

"My turn, yet?" he asked.

"Mine, actually," Sheila said, hopping up. As she started for the ball return, the hem of her tank-top snagged on the chipped edge of the table. She got three feet before Millune and I stopped her from unraveling any further.

"Well, that was almost a free show," Sheila said, grabbing up the trail of loose red thread and examining her frayed hem. "Anybody have a pair of scissors on them?"

"I got it," Vince said, casually drawing something out of his pocket. He flipped open a palm-sized object, took the thread from Sheila, and cut through it in one discreet movement.

"What was that?" Sheila all but demanded. She held her hand out to him insistently.

"Rescue knife," Vince said, handing her the refolded blade. He gave me a bewildered look then, as Millune and Elsie gathered around to gawk at the knife.

"That's right," Sheila said. "I forgot Angie told us you did the fire department thing."

"How did you get that on the plane?" I wondered aloud.

"Checked bag," Vince answered, shrugging. "You said it was kind of a long drive to the airport. I like to keep it handy, just in case." He looked uneasy when Elsie opened the blade and tapped at the serrated inner edge. "Careful. That part's for cutting through seatbelts."

Sheila stepped back from Elsie and closed the knife. She turned it over in her hand before offering it back to Vince, a scrutinizing fascination etched in her face. "Is that supposed to be a screwdriver or something?" She gestured to the rounded spike on the handle.

"Glass-breaker," Vince said, dropping the device back into his pocket. "For busting out windows and windshields."

"Okay, that's pretty sexy," Sheila said, deadpan.

"Uh...thank you?" Vince made a slow side-step toward me and away from Sheila. I almost burst out laughing at the *"Should I be worried?"* look he gave me.

"So, no brothers..." Sheila's attention was back on me. "Does he have any single friends? Preferably the hot firefighter kind—but I can be happy with just hot and Southern."

Vince now had a lost expression on his face, and I couldn't help but laugh. "I'll have to get back to you on that, Sheila."

When it came to my functionally eccentric female friends, this was probably as near to a seal of approval as I was ever going to get. I smiled to myself.

*Close enough.*

# Ever After

–

# Part 5

Nine days went by in blur.

I skipped class on Friday so my mother could take me, Vince, and my siblings to the Renaissance Festival a few towns over. It was a damp and cold day, but we all enjoyed ourselves in spite of the weather.

On the morning of our last full day together, Vince and I hardly spoke. The unease of impending separation weighed heavy on both of us. So much so, we seemed to compensate by staying in constant physical contact. The reflexive way we shadowed each other must have looked nauseatingly co-dependent. But in a way, it was more like the short period of hyperventilation before you hold your breath and dive underwater — taking in as much oxygen as possible before a long stretch of deprivation.

The weather warmed up enough in the afternoon for me to take Vince out a few miles into the country to my grandparents' farm. Together we hiked out to a spot on the edge of their land that had always been special to me: Devil's Gulch.

Deep in the woods, the water from several ravines joined together to carve out a fifty-foot sandstone precipice. It hadn't rained in a while, so the waterfall was little more than a trickle. We settled back a good fifteen feet from the ledge in a sunny clearing and watched the water drop away into the moss-walled gulch. Vince sat close at my back, his chin tucked over my left shoulder and arms wrapped around my waist.

"Are those hoof-prints?" Vince asked, pointing out a nearby set of indentations pressed into the sandy mud beside the stream.

"I think so," I said, peering intently at the widely spaced circular marks. "But they seem awfully big to be made by horse hooves. Oh! I wonder if they're from a moose."

"You have moose around here?" Vince sounded both awed and incredulous.

"Well, actually we're not supposed to have them this far south," I said, searching my memory. "Usually they're up more along the Boundary Waters Canoe Area, but sometimes they're not quite right in the head and they wander way too far south. I think it's caused by a parasite in their brains, or something like that." I scanned the tree line along the creek on the off chance I might catch sight of something moose-like. "I've never seen one close up before."

"Me neither," Vince said, voice giving a slight rise in pitch. "And I don't think I want my first encounter to involve one that's lost and crazy."

"Good point." I laughed, patting his tense arm and leaning back into him. "Don't worry about it. I don't think those are fresh tracks. And even if they are...I'm sure we'd hear something that big coming."

"Sounds like famous last words from a bad survival movie," he muttered, only partially in jest. He craned his neck side to side as if keeping on the lookout. We stayed quiet for a few minutes, straining for the sound of something large moving through the woods. Vince's hold on me gradually relaxed to something less concerned and more comfortable.

As melancholy as I was over his imminent departure, I was also content. He'd seen all he needed to, now—everything in my limited world that mattered. And he seemed all the more resolved to keep our relationship intact.

I threw him one of the few serious questions I had yet to ask him—though after all he'd put up with so far, I doubted it would scare him off. "How many kids do you want to have someday?"

"Three or four," Vince answered without pause, then cleared his throat. "I've never really been around little kids much. So...maybe just see if we can keep the first one alive and go from there." He nudged me with his chin. "How about you?"

I smiled to myself, picturing a brood of adorable red-headed children with OCD tendencies. "If they're like you, three or four sounds good."

"And if they're more like you?"

"If they're like me, God help us." I chuckled.

I expected a droll comment, but instead he lapsed back into a ponderous silence. The treetop chatter of birds and squirrels punctuated the background hiss of falling water slapping against distant rocks. Even this natural sanctuary couldn't soothe us the way I'd hoped.

I sighed finally, tired of fighting my own apprehension. "What are we going to do, Vincent?"

"I'm working on that," he murmured. When I turned my head I found his gaze calculatingly distant, fixed on some point across the gulch. "I checked my transcripts—I'm due to graduate in August of next year. When I get close, I'll put in for every entry-level position I might qualify for in Minnesota. But I haven't seen much call for my skill set up here. I don't know what to do if I can't land a decent job."

"Then I'll move to Alabama," I said, almost surprised when it came out of my mouth so easily. I knew from the start I'd considered him worth uprooting myself for, but up until now, it was more of a sentiment than a real option.

"I don't have anything to offer you, yet." Vince's chin brushed my collarbone as he shook his head. "I can't take you away from here. You have a great family, a job, some…interesting friends."

I stifled a short laugh. "Interesting friends who are about to go their separate ways. Elsie is looking at out-of-state colleges; Millune is talking about going to stay with her aunt in Georgia… And I work for a temp agency, by the way. Not exactly a locked-down commitment there." I turned my head aside more to focus on his stoic profile. "I'll get my associate degree in less than three months, and it should transfer just about anywhere. I can technically leave after December. Whenever I do decide on a career path, I'll already be halfway done."

Not for the first time I was grateful I'd been allowed to start college when I turned sixteen. Back then, college classes were a partial escape from the misery of my junior and senior year of high school. Now they meant an early sense of completion, and more importantly, freedom.

"What about your family?" He cut his eyes toward mine and I read conflict in their green depths.

"I'll miss them." I averted his gaze with the admission, hiding my trepidation over the idea of living on the opposite side of the country from everything I'd ever known. I didn't want to lay guilt on him for trying to be responsible. "It'll be hard. But not as hard as not being with you."

"This place has always been your home," Vince said, sounding unconvinced.

"That's the problem." I laughed, though there wasn't much humor in it. "I've *always* lived here. My parents have always lived here. Even my grandparents have always lived here. My parents were *neighbors*, for crying out loud. And they never got further than five miles from where they grew up." I paused to temper my restless frustration. "That's fine for them—I'm not knocking their choices. I just can't see that being…right…for me."

He seemed to process that for a moment before tentatively asking, "You think I'm right for you?"

I closed my eyes, resting my head back against his shoulder. "You feel more like home to me than any place I've ever been."

There it was.

I didn't just love him...I needed him. Not in some desperate "you complete me" sort of way. No, Vincent didn't make me whole. He improved me. Something about him—something I didn't understand—had a way of amplifying the good in my nature while muting the bad. He was a catalyst for my soul. I didn't need him in order to exist...I needed him in order to be a better *me*.

I was almost sure I did the same for him.

"We'll figure something out," Vince murmured. He lifted one hand to cup my jaw and tilted my face up. I opened my eyes to read the tender resolve in his expression. "I promise." He bent his head then and kissed me.

I twisted unconsciously until my lips fit against his with more natural leeway. What started as the warm taste of sincerity built to a mournful yearning between us. This was our unspoken "goodbye," and "until we meet again."

I didn't realize how far I'd lost myself to the moment until the heavy *snap* of a stick registered in some even more primal part of my mind. Vince froze in the same instant. A crunching noise sounded progressively closer, behind and to our left. Something was moving through the woods; something big. And it was headed straight for us.

Vince drew his face back from mine, a startled alertness inching his brows upward. His hold on me tightened, every muscle pulled taut with readiness. "Shh." He turned his face toward the disruption.

The shushing was needless. If there was some potentially dangerous animal headed for us, I had no intention of doing anything to draw its attention.

Nurturing my own sudden apprehension, I strained to make out something through the dense undergrowth around us. The brightness of our little clearing made the shadows of the surrounding forest all the more thick and ominous. There were brambles to our left, a creek-bed to our right, and a dead drop into the gulch straight ahead. Not a promising setup for any quick maneuvering.

My heart rate was already galloping, but now I could hear it thrumming in my ears. *Hey God? If we could possibly -not- be trampled to death by a crazed moose, that would be great...*

With the dry crackle of dead leaves, a shadow broke off from the trees a few yards away. My sandy-haired father stepped into view. He was carrying a rifle and accompanied by my younger brother, Tyler. "There you two are," he said, holding up his thick forearm and squinting against the sudden abundance of direct sunlight.

While I relaxed, Vince stayed wound just as tightly. I got the distinct impression he would rather be facing a charging moose than the gun-toting man whose daughter he was currently wrapped around. He started to release me and put space between us, but I stopped him. Instead he gave my father and brother an uncomfortable wave.

"Hey, Dad," I greeted, as casual as if I'd been expecting him. "Are you taking the fight to the squirrels, now?"

"Not today," he said, scouting the treetops with a sweeping blue-eyed glance. "Thinning out the cowbirds—they're a nuisance. Always laying their eggs in other bird's nests."

"Right," I said. "The deadbeat parents of the bird world." I formed an overly enthusiastic fist of solidarity, humoring him. "You guys go...give em' heck."

"Give us about an hour and we'll meet you back at grandma's," Dad said, nodding once in our general direction before moving on to jump the creek.

Tyler trailed after him, shrugging his shoulders in a helpless sort of gesture. My brother was unarmed, which meant he was likely acting as my father's bird dog. I gave him a sympathetic smile. I thought about calling after them to mention the suspicious tracks, but decided it was best not to give my dad any more ambitious hunting ideas for the day.

Once the pair had tromped on out of sight, Vince released a long sigh.

I nestled back against him, smirking over my shoulder. "You okay?"

"Just glad to be alive."

I laughed at his dramatized relief. "Staying alive *would* make it easier for us to have a future together." I paused then, humor falling away. "You know...if you're sure that's still what you want."

"I'm sure." Vince hugged me tighter to him, his voice regaining a low, serious quality that made me go still. "If I have anything to say about it, you and I have a *long* future to look forward to."

I took in his words as I melted into him. I was reasonably certain I could live off of that much reassurance, but couldn't seem to stop myself from asking, "How long?"

He pressed his lips to my temple for a lingering moment, and I knew his answer before he spoke it.

"Forever."

---------------------------------------------------------

From: Vincent
Subject: So, I was thinking and...
To: "Angeli"
Date: Tuesday, October 1, 3:14 PM

Due to our computer systems being down all day, it's been rather boring around here. So, of course, most everyone has come by to ask me about my vacation! Telling my tales to everyone gathered around, I felt something like a wise old storyteller. And apparently, I've had the greatest time in my life.

My experience with you and your family has excited everyone... telling it even excites me. People have been coming up to me all day, telling me how they enjoy my "glow" and how they can tell in my eyes that I had a wonderful time. I already knew, but it appears it is now overly official. I loved every moment I spent with you.

Sitting here, looking at your picture on my wall, I am reminded how much I /did/ enjoy being with you. I miss you entirely too much, my Angel.

So, I was thinking and... just thought I'd write to say: "I love you."

Forever,
--Vincent

---------------------------------------------------------

*November 16th,*

*I've neglected this journal for far too long. Though perhaps its allowed, since I only intended it to be for my road trip. My life trip is far from over, however.*

*It has been an excruciating 48 days since Vincent came up to stay with me and my family. I have another 34 left to endure.*

*I want to be with him, and even as he's gotten to know me so well, he still wants to be with me. The strain of our situation demands that we find a way to be near each other. For a time at least, it looks like I will be the one to relocate. I'm making peace with that idea.*

*I know we both want to spend our lives together, but when exactly that will be arranged or officialized, I can't say. I know Vincent has been made to feel too young for making any serious plans, and perhaps I should consider myself, also. But I truly believe that, with God's help, we can make this relationship work. And work well.*

*Odd, how life makes twists and turns. I never would have guessed that I'd end up where I am now, but I wouldn't trade it for the world. I wouldn't trade this path I'm on for the whole solar system, for that matter. If I've learned anything these last several months, it's that sometimes the most scenic roads in life are the detours you didn't mean to take.*

*~Ang*

# Breaking Up Is Hard To Do
-
## Part 1

Airfare for the week of Thanksgiving turned out to be about a dollar short of a back-alley mugging. I couldn't safely afford a plane ticket and still be sure I could fly down to Alabama for two weeks over Christmas. And being stubbornly independent, I wasn't about to let Vince pay for my ticket. *We can wait an extra month to see each other,* I reasoned. Four more weeks on top of the six we'd already been apart. It would be hard, but we could do it.

Vince was less confident in his ability to endure. I had to resort to reminding him that his car needed repairs before he would promise not to drive or fly up to Minnesota over the holiday. He still seemed a bit sulky the week before Thanksgiving break. On one particular day he let me know he'd be late in calling me, as he'd been roped into acting as the designated driver for a handful of his college friends. I encouraged him to go. He spent so much of his free time on the phone with me, I was afraid I'd inadvertently snuffed out his social life. I hoped a little "guy time" would cheer him up.

As it turned out, my hope was misplaced.

The phone rang a little after 11:30 that Thursday evening. In the middle of a charcoal self-portrait for my Life Drawing class, I grabbed the phone with my least blackened hand and answered on the first ring.

"Congratulations, you've just won a *free* cruise to the Bahamas," I announced in my best over-cheerful telemarketer voice. "Please have your credit card or bank account number ready."

"Hey, babe," Vince said, his tone impassive. Judging by the muffled wind-like drone in the background, he was still driving. "What're you up to?"

That didn't bode well. Normally he'd at least indulge my lame attempts at being funny.

"Besides no good?" I frowned at myself in the little round mirror that sat on the corner of my desk. My face was already covered in dark smudges. I considered including them in the sketch, but decided it might raise questions from my classmates. "Just finishing up some art homework. Currently, I think I'm wearing more of my medium than the paper is."

"Ah," he said, voice gaining more warmth. Maybe he was just tired. "So you're finally drawing something other than naked people and chairs?"

"Actually…I'm drawing myself," I said, putting my best effort into a sultry voice. "And I just happen to be sitting in a chair…"

His breath hitched, and I couldn't help but laugh. I hadn't thought my teasing would work. "It's just a portrait—sorry to disappoint," I clarified, absently gauging the differences between the two dark irises I had down on my sketch paper. "Did you have a good time with your friends?"

Vince blew out a long breath. "Yeah, I guess so."

"What's wrong?" I asked. "Did somebody puke in your car?"

"No," he said, his voice mellowing to its usual tenor. "Nobody overdid it too bad this time."

"Oh, well good." I paused, "Did somebody hit on you and you don't want to tell me about it because you're afraid I'll be psychotically jealous?"

"Huh?"

He sounded distracted, so I pressed on, trying to goad the truth out of him. "Ooo…was it a guy?"

"Wait…what? No." His voice wavered with resolving confusion. "Nobody hit on me."

Clearly I was failing at lightening his mood.

"Okay," I said, setting down my charcoal stick. I closed my eyes and poured my full attention into picturing how his face would match his tonal nuances. "So what's the matter, then?"

"It's nothing," he said, taking a little too long to answer. "It's not important."

Concern gnawed at my stomach. In my mind's eye I could see his reddish brows knit together, pensive green eyes shrouded by nighttime shadows. He was definitely bothered. "Truth oath," I said, reminding him of our pact to never keep anything from each other.

It was a trump card. Normally he was the one holding it over me, extracting all troublesome thoughts from my over-analytical brain before they festered into some overblown monstrosity that neither of us should have to slay. But this time it was him holding back, and I wanted to know why.

I heard him take in a slow breath of preparation. "We got to talking, that's all. Some of the guys were asking about you."

I shifted my weight, the chair under me suddenly uncomfortable. "Have I met any of them?"

"No," Vince answered, still sounding distracted. "Nobody from that class you visited over the summer. They only heard about that whole *incident* later."

"Okay, so nobody who watched me end up in a headlock and almost die. That's encouraging, at least..." I rubbed at my forehead, trying to soothe away the unpleasant memory. "So, what were they asking about me?"

"Basic stuff," he said, more of an aversion than an answer. "Where you're from...what you're in school for...how I ended up with a Yankee girl—that kind of thing."

"Ugh," I grumped. "Do I really have to be considered a Yankee? Minnesota was barely a state when the civil war happened."

"I don't come up with the cultural nuances, I just try my best to ignore them," Vince said, the hint of a smirk in his voice. "Anyways, they wanted to know how serious it was. So I told them we were talking about getting married."

My stomach fluttered, and warmth flooded my chest. "You did?" We tended to talk about marriage on and off as an inevitability. But as far as I knew, this was the first time he'd announced his intentions to anyone else. Something about that made it feel more real and less like distant speculation. Still, caution rode hard on the heels of my elation. "What...did they have to say about that?"

An uncomfortable silence stretched out between us. I waited, counting my own thudding heartbeats.

"They, uh—" Vince cleared his throat. "—wanted to know if I'd test-driven the car before I bought it. I told them no..."

All warmth fled my chest, as though my heart had been dipped in a bucket of ice. "Test-driven *the car*?" I repeated, unable to choose between disbelief and blooming anger. Sarcasm bit its way into my voice, "Sorry...would I be wrong to assume that was a crappy metaphor for "have you slept with her yet to make sure she's worth the trouble?"

More uneasy silence. "They didn't mean it as bad as it sounds—"

"Well good, because it sounds terrible!" I shot back, unable to curb my own snappishness. "It's always *so* humanizing to be compared to the purchase of an inanimate object."

He groaned out a sigh. "See, that's why I didn't want to talk about it."

"Why?" I asked, trying to calm my voice. "Because you didn't want me to know your friends are a herd of asses...or because you're actually starting to agree with them?" Calmness failed me and the question came out in a gush of wounded indignation.

"Look, I know how it sounds," he said, putting forth the negotiating voice I normally heard him use on his mother or unruly clients at work. It only stoked my irritation. "But believe it or not, they were genuinely concerned about me. They also brought up some good points."

"Such as?" I pushed my desk chair back and stood so I could pace my bedroom. My agitation needed some sort of physical outlet, and punching something wasn't an option.

"Such as...what if it turns out we're not compatible?"

"Not compatible, how?" I asked, mystified. "Look, I may not have prior experience, but I do have a pretty solid grasp of anatomy. Insert tab A into slot B—it doesn't take a genius to figure out. So unless you're a eunuch and you decided not to tell me, I'm failing to see how we could *not* be physically compatible." I paused, calming enough to file the edges off my tone. "And honestly, it wouldn't matter to me if you were a eunuch. I can work with that. There's always adoption, if you still want kids..."

"Angie," Vince said, with a tinge of exasperation. "I'm definitely *not* a eunuch."

"Okay, I'll take your word for it." I tried to smile but failed. "Then what's the alleged problem?"

When Vince spoke again, his voice lowered, "How do you know you won't be one of those women who don't like sex?"

"I'm pretty confident that won't be a problem—"

"But you don't know," he emphasized, with quiet precision. "You don't know how bad that whole thing with Scott might have affected you."

*That whole thing with Scott.*

The words struck me like a low blow to the gut. He meant the nightmares—the post-traumatic stress symptoms. He meant the fact that I was still damaged from nearly being raped by a friend I once thought I could trust.

I doubled forward, hot tears welling up and spilling down my cheeks before I even thought to suppress them. I stared down at the plush, ocean blue carpet under my bare feet and hugged one arm around my middle. "Maybe I don't," I said at last, hearing the waver in my own voice. "But I've been getting better. If I need to, I'll get counseling."

"It isn't just that." Vince sounded strained, but if he realized how bad he'd hurt me, he didn't let on. "I've been thinking a lot lately. I know how important you think it is to wait for marriage and all, but to me it just seems like you don't trust me. You know I mean to marry you eventually... When there's money for it, and I'm not living with my parents anymore. I'm trying to do this the right way, but it's like I'm being punished in the meantime."

It sounded like an accusation, and it stung. I sucked in a steadying breath. "You're not being punished. I don't know what kind of ideas your *friends* might have put in your head, but I'm not some horrible prude who plans on using sex as some sort of weapon against you. I explained this before we were ever together. I decided a long time ago I wanted to save that part of myself as a gift...for my husband."

*For you, I thought...*

"Yeah, well, I guess I'm used to opening my gifts early," Vince said, so low I almost didn't hear him. He released a pained sigh. "I love you, Angel. I'm not going to just use you and then leave you. Why can't you take my word for it?"

My heart flinched. Somehow, I felt much like I had as a small child. I had the sudden and vivid recollection of a long-forgotten instance — when I'd presented my father with the most unique rock I'd ever found, and he'd been too impatient to humor me. I'd felt this same kind of mournful ache all those years ago. It was the dull realization that something I considered precious and beautiful might, in fact, be worthless to the one person I most wanted to give it to.

"I didn't make the rules, I'm just trying to follow them as best I can." I dragged a palm down my face, uselessly wiping at the flow of tears that hadn't slowed. My voice sounded as ragged as my throat felt. "I'm trying to do this the right way too, Vince. I'm not abstinent because I enjoy saying no to you. I told you from the start what my boundaries were, and you agreed to respect them. Are you…changing your mind now, just because your friends had a few drinks and decided they were relationship experts?"

*Not to mention car experts,* I thought, bitterly.

"I didn't say I'd changed my mind," Vince said, his exasperation mounting. "I'm just…taking a step back to look at this from a different angle, that's all."

"What angle?" I asked, reigning in the defensiveness that threatened to tint my voice with scorn. Before he could answer, I put forth another question in as reasonable a tone as I could manage, "And how many of these *concerned* friends of yours are actually in some kind of healthy, functional relationship?"

Vince was silent for a long while. I'd thought my question was valid—maybe he'd found some sense in it. Then again, he might not see it as any more than an attack on his friends. I knew his sense of loyalty ran deep. Up until now, I'd never questioned it. But if those friends had made me out to be some sort of hyper-religious control freak...

I waited out his reaction with mounting dread.

"It's not just them that think you're being unreasonable," he said, with such quiet reservation I couldn't picture any facial expression of his that might fit it. The uncertainty carved out a hole through the middle of me. "I just talked to Grady about it a few days ago."

"Grady?" I murmured. A numb sense of betrayal crept in to fill the vacuum.

Grady had been Vince's best friend since early high school. I'd met him several times over the summer when I'd stopped off on my road trip to visit Vince, and I still had a clear recollection of the dark-haired, charismatic young man. Out of everyone Vince was close to, Grady's opinion meant the most to him.

Now, it sounded as though Grady's opinion had somehow turned against me.

"Grady said it shouldn't be a big deal." Vince began, his voice gaining conviction. "He said as long as we plan on getting married, it doesn't matter when we decide to start sleeping together. And I mean…his dad is a deacon. That has to count for something."

"To me, all that counts for is Grady justifying something *he* wants to do," I said through gritted teeth. "I'm willing to bet he didn't run that little bit of advice past his dad or his pastor first."

Vince was silent on his end for a long while. The only sound I picked up on was the opening and closing of his car door, followed by the creak of wooden stairs. He must have made it home. A tiny part of me was relieved. If we were going to have a fight, I didn't want him behind the wheel.

"He's like my brother," Vince said at last, defensive. "He wouldn't steer me wrong on purpose."

"I'm not saying he did it on purpose." I softened my voice as much as I could, considering my running nose and the steady onslaught of tears that clogged my throat. "Vince, I don't doubt you *intend* to marry me one day. You have a lot of good intentions, but you know…there's also a reason they say the road to Hell is paved with those." I paused, willing him to understand. A still-raw analogy drifted to the forefront of my mind and out of my mouth. "You *intended* to always be with your ex-girlfriend, too. But it didn't turn out that way."

*And this is all part of the aftermath.*

I had no doubt that most of Vince's current impatience came back down to him knowing what he was missing. It wasn't fair, but it was a foreseeable pothole on this road I'd chosen to take with him.

"That was her decision, not mine." Vince's voice hardened. He didn't have many nerves to hit, but it was clear I'd just taken a sledgehammer to the worst of them. "So the bottom line is…you still don't trust me to keep my word and not back out of this. You won't trust me until I sign some stupid piece of paper."

"I'm not saying that!" I choked on a sob, unable to keep the shuddering out of my words any longer. He was angry with me. I was so used to him defusing me—or at least affably enduring my volatility—I didn't know what to do with the knowledge that I'd finally earned his disdain. I had to make him understand.

"Vince, I love you. Heart, mind, soul…and body." I squeezed my leaking eyes shut, articulating the order of my words with agonizing deliberateness. "I will marry you, if you ask. I will leave my family and move to Alabama, if you ask. But please…please don't ask me to choose what you want over my relationship with God. You'll lose."

"You have to admit," Vince spoke in a weighty tone, as though he hadn't processed my heartfelt words at all. "It's not exactly normal. This isn't how it works with most people."

*Not exactly normal.* My mind blistered as the words seared through my thoughts.

"I'm not most people. *We're* not most people," I told him, tears stripping my voice of dignity. A deep ache permeated my chest. Pushing back against the pain, the beginnings of a rant rose up within me and came out in a fuming rush, "Anyway, it's a little late to be mad at me for defying something mainstream society currently considers acceptable. A couple hundred years ago, "normal" involved hoopskirts and chaperones. A hundred years from now, "normal" could involve aliens and cybernetic implants. I don't know. But I do know I didn't hide any of my standards or *abnormalities* from you. I figured they would scare you off early on, but they didn't. You even claimed you *liked* how different I am."

"Yeah, well, there's no accounting for taste." Vince's voice came out as little more than a grim mutter. "I guess…I miscalculated how well I could handle all of this."

*Oh, ouch.*

My chest tightened as I stumbled to the foot of my bed. I sank down and let the mattress steady me, since my legs weren't willing to do the job anymore. He didn't even sound like my Vincent. After all of these past weeks and months—endless hours of soul-bearing and talking things out—how could I have missed this part of him?

"Well then," I whispered, stifling another sob and hating myself over how much anguish slipped through. "It's a good thing you haven't signed some stupid piece of paper."

"Look, I'm really tired," he said, voice thick with weary aggravation. "I've got a lot to think about. I'm going to let you go, okay?"

"Okay." I swallowed, tears pricking afresh behind the bridge of my nose. He was letting me go? He meant from the phone conversation, of course, but the wording of it struck me like a runaway truck. The discord between us had shaken my confidence to the point where I wasn't sure what he truly meant. "Good night, Vincent."

"Good night," Vince echoed. All sound on the other end cut off.

Stunned, I waited a few seconds before pulling the phone away from my head. I stared down at it and then brought it back to my ear. "Vince?"

Nothing.

He'd hung up.

Worse, he'd hung up without saying "I love you."

As inane as it might have been, I realized at that moment how comforting I found the ritual. Since the day I'd agreed to us trying out a real relationship, Vince had ended every call with the same affirmation. Even in those first days, when I couldn't yet bring myself to return the sentiment. Good day or bad day, he'd never failed to make those his last words to me.

Until now.

I waited, incredulous. Surely he'd realize what he'd done. Or rather, *not* done.

I stared at my phone, minutes passing like hours. Finally I forced myself to stand and shuffle back to my desk. My self-portrait stared back at me, eyes glazed and lifeless. Ironically, this was probably the most accurate realism I'd ever achieved. A glance in the mirror confirmed my wretched-looking state.

I reached out and dragged my damp fingertips down the middle of my represented face, smearing the newsprint. On impulse, I scrawled out a title in the bottom corner of the sketch:

*Girl Who Just Got Dumped*

# Breaking Up Is Hard To Do
## -
## Part 2

In the morning, I awoke feeling as though my 45-pound dog must be sitting on my chest.

She wasn't.

I stared up at the ceiling, counting phosphorescent plastic stars as I replayed the fight with Vincent over and over. My head throbbed and my eyes were swollen. Dried salt clung to my cheeks, just as my mind clung to a strange bewilderment over how much pain I was in.

*So, this is what it's like.*

I'd been so careful with love, and still it ended up crushing me. Now, all of those miserable physical symptoms of heartache—the ones I'd read about and observed in others, but always questioned—were proving their legitimacy with a vengeance.

I considered spending the day curled up with a quart of ice cream, but decided that sounded too much like conceding defeat. Instead, I rolled out of bed and stared into my closet with an appalling lack of motivation. The fact that I was about to be late for my first morning class didn't have the slightest effect on me. I knew I should be rushing, checking off the day's responsibilities as I went, but apathy held me like slow, sucking quicksand. All I could think about was Vince.

*This is ridiculous. You're being ridiculous,* I scolded myself.

My dog, Haley, nudged the bedroom door open and stuck her head in. Her long muzzle relaxed in a lazy canine smile, ears half-cocked in inquiry. I called her to me and knelt, burying my face in the shaggy Collie mane of her neck. "Did you know I needed a hug?" I murmured, grounding myself in her smell. Unwashed animal fur and dying grass—she needed a bath.

I kissed Haley's head between her ears and released her. The simple contact took a tiny bit of the weight off of me. Enough that I worked up the gumption to throw on clean jeans and a Spiderman T-shirt, completing my frumpy-yet-practical college student look. I tended to my rats next, numbly going through the routine of feeding and petting them. Priscilla licked my hand, her buggy black eyes seeming to peer straight through me. I scooped her up and brought her to my cheek to nuzzle.

*Pet therapy definitely has some merit*, I thought, placing the gentle rodent back in her cage. It was too bad I couldn't bring her with me to class.

The idea occurred to me then that some human interaction might bring some relief as well. But who could I talk to? I wasn't close to my sister, and I couldn't stomach the idea of telling my Mom I'd been wrong about Vince…not yet, anyway.

I would just have to suck it up and take the day one hour at a time.

Sucking it up amounted to me dragging my feet throughout the morning when all I wanted was to crawl under something and stare off into space. First I was late to my Creative Writing class, where I couldn't hope to concentrate on the assignment. When I finally left I didn't remember anything I'd written. I hoped I wouldn't later discover I'd put some poor TA through the unfortunate task of grading my awful, angst-ridden poetry.

My Life Drawing class went nearly as bad. I had enough foresight to scratch out the title of my self-portrait and attempt to clean it up before the professor got around to me. It was a demanding class—I expected a poor grade after deliberately marring the piece. But instead, my professor considered it a long while before nodding and marking a small A- on the back corner.

"I know it's not very good," I murmured, arguing with her judgment aloud before I could stop myself. Normally I had the utmost respect for her. I'd fought hard to make it into this class because I had so much admiration for her talents and perspective. But at that exact moment, the aching tension behind my ribs had me convinced that *everything* in the world was wrong. Including the most brilliant artist I'd ever met.

The petite woman stopped, tilting her head as she looked up at me with her dark, unfathomable eyes. She looked for so long I had to wonder if she was seeing me as a collection of lines and planes, lights and darks. "It's truth," she said at last, laying a frail, weathered hand on my arm. "Don't apologize when it comes out in your work."

She moved on then, leaving me with the sense that she'd seen something I might never comprehend.

When the class was over—what felt like a decade later—I threw away my portrait. Not because I disagreed with the grade, but because I wanted to get rid of every emotion I now attached to that work. I longed to discard the desolate part of me that wouldn't allow any feeling but aching grief—grief for what was, and for what could have been. Grief over losing the best friend I'd ever had.

*God, this hurts.*

I spent my noon break sitting beside the fountain in front of the Student Union, shivering in the late November air. The day was damp and dreary, as if mimicking my mood.

Silently, I asked forgiveness for every person whose personal heartbreak I might ever have disregarded. There had to be a less painful way to learn empathy.

I wanted to be angry. Anger seemed so much more reasonable and productive. The guy I'd placed so much hope and faith in had rejected me—allowed his devotion to be swayed by immature, hormone-driven friends. Whatever happened to "You're worth the wait" and "Sex isn't love"? What happened to the sweet, selfless guy I'd been willing to bet my whole future on?

Every plan and promise we'd made, all for nothing.

I couldn't even manage anger. Hollow disappointment seemed my only constant, along with a nagging sense of worry. I couldn't help but wonder what would become of Vince now that he was free of me. Would it be easy for him to cover over all memories of us with some other, more "normal" girl? Would he ever regret letting me go?

...would he be okay?

I touched the center of my small cross pendant—the one Vince had sent me the day I'd come home from my road trip. The day I'd finally let myself love him. I wound the necklace chain around my fingers and closed my fist, but that was as close as I could get to taking it off. It was the best reminder I had that our relationship *wasn't* all for nothing. He might have hurt me in the end, but I couldn't forget how much he'd helped me to heal.

*Please...please take care of him,* I prayed.

Struggling to distract myself, I plotted out the next few months in my head. I had finals and graduation all in less than three weeks—assuming I could pull myself together enough to limp across that academic finish line. I would claim my Associate's degree and take time off to figure things out, just as I'd originally planned. Come spring, I could save up money and take off on another long road trip—this time to the West Coast. But no guys this time around…no unforeseen, complicated relationships.

My hands itched to grip a steering wheel and feel the dim vibration of an engine through my palms. I could do it again—just me, God, and the open road. Wanderlust was making a sudden and compelling return.

Or maybe that was just the urge to run away.

~ ~ ~ ~ ~ ~ ~

My afternoon statistics class lasted for approximately a century.

On a normal day, few things failed to hold my interest like numbers. On that particular day, I might as well have spent the hour staring at hieroglyphics while juggling my slide into melancholy. My one consolation was that there wasn't a pop quiz.

I decided it must be true what my mother used to tell me: I wore my heart on my face. My classmates started asking if I was okay. I wasn't. I knew I would be, eventually. I just wasn't sure how to hurry up the process.

Couldn't I skip the severely depressed phase and move on to being sulky-yet-purposeful?

I didn't want to go home after class. I wanted to feel better—or at least, more tolerable—before I faced my family. Aikido would have been a good outlet, but the club didn't meet on Thursdays. I considered going to see Elsie, but knew I wouldn't find any semblance of compassionate understanding there. Personal discussions made her itchy—and it didn't get much more personal than this.

I meant to drive around town aimlessly, but somehow ended up on my friend Sheila's doorstep. She showed me to the basement game room before disappearing, saying something about making a snack run. Downstairs I found Elsie sprawled out on one end of a ratty sofa, her short russet hair forming an untamed mop around her face as she poured her focus into a vintage Nintendo game. Millune occupied the overstuffed suede lounger across the room, alternating between watching Elsie's game and studying for her citizenship test.

Millune looked up first. I wasn't surprised to see her anywhere but her own home. With nine wild younger siblings and a mother who loathed everyone who wasn't Somali, her house wasn't even close to being a comfortable environment. "Hey, Angie...are you sick?" she asked.

"Kind of," I answered, shuffling toward the sofa.

*Heartsick.* I understood that term, now.

Elsie scooted further to her own side of the sofa, making excessive room for me while never taking her eyes off the TV screen. "Well, don't give it to me. I have to retake the ACT this Saturday," she griped in a disinterested tone.

"Don't worry," I muttered, dropping facedown onto the two cushions she'd left me. I grabbed up a throw pillow and hugged it to my chest, as though it might work as a splint for my injured heart. "It's not contagious." If I'd come to distract myself from thinking about Vince, the backdrop of video game music wasn't helping. But at least I wasn't completely alone.

I stared, unfocused, at the TV screen for several minutes before Millune's face broke into my line of sight. She knelt to sit primly in front of me, her smooth, heart-shaped face tilted in inquiry. "Did somebody die?"

Her unwitting bluntness deserved a smile, but amusement seemed beyond me. "I look that bad, huh?"

Millune nodded, her dark brows tight with concern.

"No. No death," I said. With a sigh, I decided it was as good a time as any to test the admission, "Vince broke up with me."

"Oh, no..." Millune gasped, drawing her head back. Her voice fell to a soft, mournful pitch. "I thought he was so smart."

"Thanks." I snorted, rubbing my face against the pillow I clutched to fend off the threatening pinpricks of tears. I was done with crying. Ranting had to be a better option.

I recited the cliff notes from our fight the night before, managing more calmness than I'd anticipated. Saying it all out loud made me feel moderately better over standing my ground. Millune's head-shaking look of disbelief didn't hurt, either.

"That's terrible," Millune lamented. She gave my hand an awkward little pat. "If he had such problems with your beliefs, he should have dumped you *much* sooner."

I forced a short laugh. As oddly as she'd phrased it, I couldn't disagree with the assessment.

"That's guys for you," Elsie said, distractedly. She'd moved on to another level, but didn't pause the game as she spoke. "They start listening to their stupid friends, and then they start *doing* stupid things. That's how Alan got arrested that last time..." she cursed under her breath as her character died, then dropped the console controller on the floor in front of her. "You're better off, though," she went on, finally casting her grey-blue gaze my way. "I mean, who wants to be with a guy that weak-willed?"

"Not helping, Elsie," I said.

"Sorry." She was quiet for a few beats, and then offered, "I hope some rebound slut gives him herpes?"

"Elsie!" Millune and I called out in warning at the same time.

"Okay, okay...that was harsh," she conceded. "Maybe just a moderately bad case of crabs. That one's treatable, right?"

I wound back and whipped the throw pillow at Elsie's head. She squawked, flailing dramatically as she fell off the couch. "I'm hit!"

"Why did I even come here?" I sighed, dropping my head back against the couch arm.

Elsie looked up from her new location on the worn taupe carpet and shrugged. "Hey, I'm just trying to help. This isn't exactly my area of expertise." She curled herself around the game controller and used it to flip through a menu screen.

Millune tugged at her hair in worried thought, twisting the tight black coils around her fingers. "What...can we do?"

I reached out and squeezed her shoulder, appreciation thawing some of my listlessness.

"You're already doing it. Just...let me hang out a while, and don't let me wallow in self-pity."

Still looking perplexed, Millune gave a slow nod. "Wallowing is for pigs, not for Angies."

This time my laugh was real. "That sounds about right."

I stayed for a few hours, growing more comfortable once Sheila returned with food and Elsie left for work. After Millune filled Sheila in on the situation, the two girls managed to keep the conversation distractingly mundane. I eventually scraped myself off the couch long enough to visit the computer in the back corner of the game room.

It was then I found an email from Vince in my inbox, dated from 7:30 AM that morning. I jumped up without opening it or even reading the subject line. The correspondence could only be one of two things: further justification for the rightness of his argument...or an apology. I wasn't sure I wanted to face either of those things.

"What happened?" Millune called from somewhere behind me. "You look like the computer bite you."

"Bit," Sheila said, offering the linguistic correction automatically. "Past-tense."

I didn't answer at first. Instead I turned away and walked a few laps around the sofa, trying to pull my thoughts together. If Vince was only continuing the fight from the night before, I couldn't stand to read it. If he was trying to apologize...I was afraid I wouldn't believe him. There was no way we could have a sustainable relationship if his friends' opinions meant more to him than mine. And even if we made up, how long would it last before he got tired of waiting again?

Sheila looked up from the movie she'd been watching and peered at me over the top of her vintage glasses, bland annoyance written all over her pallid face. "Are you gonna tell us what's up, or are you just wearing holes in the floor for the sheer joy of it?"

"I need you guys to do me a favor," I said, stopping to look from Millune to Sheila. "Vince emailed me. Come have a look and tell me if I should actually read it, or just trash it before it makes me any more unstable than I already am."

Both girls perked up and glanced at each other. With a near-simultaneous nod, they got up and drifted over to the computer. "No problem," Sheila said over her shoulder. "If it's bad enough, we'll delete it for you."

"Thanks," I muttered, finding the end of the sofa and sinking down against the arm to wait for their verdict. "I think I trust just about anybody's judgment more than mine right now."

I waited. Trepidation ran tight and jittery through my chest, like an overstretched rubber band. I wasn't sure what would happen when the tension finally broke. I only knew it seemed like a prolonged stint of silence before Millune's voice called my attention back toward the computer.

"Hey, Angie?" Her voice wobbled. "You should come read this."

I stood, heart rate spiking as I made my way back. Whatever I might have expected, it threw me off completely to gauge the reaction of both girls as they backed away from the computer screen. Sheila took off her glasses, looking embarrassed as she brushed away tears. Millune alternated between biting her upper and lower lip, looking like she was barely holding herself together.

Curiosity blotted out my leeriness with a sudden intensity. I sat in the computer chair and scooted close, reading first the subject line. It was made up of just one word: Eternity. I began the letter then, my head immediately filling with Vincent's contrite tenor voice.

Hello, My Love.

As I sit here, I can't help but wonder if I will be the cause of you having a terrible day today. I wonder if I will have caused a dark cloud to settle over your head and follow you throughout the day. And as I wonder this, I grow sad. I hate the thought. I hate the idea that you might be unhappy because of our talk last night. But I know it's very probable. I know I am unhappy.

But you must know, Angel, that I cannot stand to see you sad. In your unhappiness, there stands a broken heart in my chest. I want to live for you. I want to be everything for you. I want us to be forever and eternity. You cannot know how precious you are to me. And I do not wish to fracture a fragile soul.

I pray that you get this before your day starts, but I do not know that you will. Angeli, please smile and laugh and be happy. Don't worry about the guys around here and the thoughts they put in my head. I don't care anymore. I don't. I just want to make you happy—and I think I know what I must do to make that happen.

"I love you heart, mind, soul, and body." I say to you what you said to me. Every ounce of me (though few ounces there may be) is infatuated with you. And I don't dare try to analyze or explain this constant, exciting passion that drives me. Every minute that I spend without you only fuels my burning desire to hold you in my arms and love you as God intended you to be loved. Every minute I spend with you on the phone I grow anxious for the hour I finally get to be with you again, and I crave to hear that voice as I see your lips move.

Yes, I am in love. I am in love with an Angel of God. A creation more precious than this Earth and more beautiful than the day's sunset. I know a rose cannot explain my feelings, nor can six. I sent them, though, so that you would know I will not sit idly by while my heart exists so far from my chest. I love you, and I will reach you. Space cannot separate you from me, and neither can the words of others.

Do not distress, Angel. I could not see, but just hearing you cry was like being stabbed relentlessly in the heart without the ability to die...just suffering. I can't take that anymore, Angel. I can't handle you being unhappy. It hurts me. I will do anything for you, and you should know that. If you're hurting, I want you to tell me. I want you to talk to me, especially if you're feeling hurt or uncomfortable. I have to know, Baby. I want to assure you that I have not changed any of my plans, and I love you more than the day I met you.

I love you, Angel. I love you so much. That's not going to change. You will forever be a part of me, and thus a part of my life. Please smile for me, Angel. Never stop smiling for me.

Forever your love,
-Vincent
XOXOXO

I reread the letter, letting Vince's words wash over and fill the cracks in my heart. I believed him. I couldn't help but believe him.

My external awareness came trickling back and I glanced around. Sheila and Millune hadn't gone far. Millune clasped her hands before her, looking at me with a wistful smile. Sheila had dried up and crossed her arms, pulling off her best stoic-girl impression.

"I need to go," I said.

"Yes, you do," Millune agreed. "You have some stupid to forgive."

"If you decide you don't want them, I'll take the flowers," Sheila said, straight-faced as ever. "Same goes for the poetic boyfriend."

"Thanks." I smiled. "But I think I'll be keeping both."

# Forever

On December 20th, Vince picked me up at the Atlanta airport and drove us back to his parent's house in Cropwell, Alabama.

It was a surreal drive for me. Not only was I thrilled to be with Vince again, but I was returning to a place that — five months earlier — I'd been so certain I'd never see again. The warm weather seemed to amplify the strangeness. The temperature was in the low 60's — a solid 50-degree disparity from the tundra-like conditions I'd left back in Minnesota just a few hours earlier.

"Miss the cold, yet?" Vince glanced aside from the driver's seat and smirked.

"Not even a little bit." I smirked back. "It's going to be weird though, not seeing snow on Christmas. But I think I can get used to it."

*I could get used to never seeing snow at all,* I wanted to add. But that seemed needy. Instead I squeezed his hand, tightening the interweaving of our fingers.

Aside from occasional turns and bouts of high-stress traffic, he'd held my hand through the entire 2-hour trek. I didn't mind in the slightest. After more than ten weeks apart, it felt wrong for us to be in the same place and *not* touching.

"I'll try to make it worth it," Vince said, voice mild and serious as he scanned the road ahead. He was thinking hard about something, and I knew it wasn't driving. "So…I feel the need to warn you," he began, breaking the lull before I could ask him what was wrong. "My dad wants to have some kind of…talk…with both of us. He'll be home when we get there."

"Oh, so I'll finally get to meet him." I tried to sound cheerful about it, but the tense set of Vince's copper brows had me concerned. He was uneasy, and that made *me* uneasy. "Any idea what he wants to talk about?"

Vince shook his head, green gaze flitting my way and back to the road. "Not a clue. He called while I was on my way to get you and wanted to know when he could expect us—wouldn't tell me what was up."

I sifted through the mental cache of information I'd gathered on Vince's dad since we'd first met. I recalled the wedding photo I'd studied while snooping…er…browsing on my first and only visit, but the image of the rail-thin, mustached youth was twenty years out of date. What else did I know about the man who was potentially about to interrogate me?

His name was Cecil. Like my dad, he had a well-used workshop, the compulsion to tinker, and a penchant for outdoorsman activities of all kinds. Unlike my dad, he enjoyed country music and hanging out in bars. I also had the distinct impression that he and Vince had precious little in common outside of blood and living space.

I took a deep breath and let the obvious insecure question fly, "Do you think...he'll like me?"

Vince's thumb massaged the back of my hand, his almost too-full lips twitching into a smile. "I don't see how he couldn't."

Sweet. Not a straight answer, but sweet.

"I'm an acquired taste," I pointed out, skeptical.

"Well," Vince glanced my way again and raised his brows. "As I recall, I acquired that taste pretty fast."

It was a fleeting look of intensity, but it was enough to heat my insides. Good thing I wasn't one to blush. I turned my face to stare out the window and watch the still-lush forests rush past. "Four days," I spoke the thought before I'd realized it. It still sounded crazy, even out loud. He'd decided he loved me after just four days of seeing me in person. It was especially bizarre if one didn't count the years we'd known each other as faceless internet personalities—escaping reality through stories and characters of our own design.

Vince seemed to understand before I could elaborate. "Two days, actually."

I looked back at him in surprise. His gaze was fixed on the road, but his thoughts were elsewhere. "When I had that big come-apart moment and you prayed for me. Didn't feel sorry for me, just...cared. I knew then." He flashed an embarrassed half-smile. "I waited a couple of days to make sure. And, you know, not scare you off."

"Oh, that went well, didn't it?" I snickered. I could find it funny now, but the confusion and emotional upheaval of that time were fresh in my memory. It still amazed me how we'd somehow built a strong relationship from such peculiar beginnings.

"I've had better ideas," he admitted. "I don't blame you for not believing me. I wouldn't have believed me if I wasn't...*me*." He paused as he seemed to review how much sense his last sentence had made. As if to distract from it, he lifted my hand and pressed a kiss to the back of it. "I'm glad you gave us a chance."

"I'm glad you were persistent," I said, leaning aside until I could rest my temple against his shoulder.

I'd almost forgotten any anxiety over meeting his dad when I realized we were pulling into his parent's driveway. Fallen pecans from overhanging trees crunched softly under the car's tires as I sat up, taking in the distantly familiar yellow house nestled back in the corner of a dense tree line. Vince pulled up to park beside a black pickup truck and got out to take my bags from the trunk.

Still unused to having anything done for me, I fidgeted off to one side while he loaded himself down like a pack mule. For some reason I'd packed twice as much luggage for this two week visit than I'd brought on my entire two-month road trip.

"Sorry. I promise I'm not becoming high-maintenance."

Vince flashed me an easy grin. "Don't worry about it. You should see how my mom packs for just a weekend."

I followed him inside and up the creaking wooden steps to the living room, where his dad met us.

"So, you're the one who flew in under my radar," Cecil said, without preamble. His voice fell a few notches lower than Vince's and carried a gruff drawl.

"Yes...sir?" I said, looking to Vince for help on how to read his father. But Vince only murmured a quick introduction and ducked down the hallway to deposit my bags. I faced those few seconds of abandonment the only way I could think to—I offered out a handshake.

Cecil was about Vince's height, lean in both face and stature. But that was where the similarities ended. Tattoos spotted his upper arms and disappeared under a gray T-shirt, which featured the image of a largemouth bass leaping from a patch of water poised level with his slight beer gut. Graying sideburns peeked out from under a tattered camouflage baseball cap. His eyes were a sharp shade of light blue, granting him a keen and decisive appearance. He carried himself with the rigid confidence I expected from a former military serviceman.

The man gave me a sweeping look of assessment and accepted my hand, administering a firm squeeze with the shake. On reflex I answered by gripping a small degree tighter than he had, not releasing until I felt him first relax his dry, calloused hold. I wondered then if I'd just inadvertently challenged my boyfriend's father to some sort of redneck duel.

I decided I should soften the first-impression with gratitude. "Thank you for letting me stay here...again."

Cecil scrubbed a thumb and forefinger along his clean-shaven chin, eyeing me with something like perplexed contemplation. "I'm still tryin' to figure how I missed you the first time," he said, more matter-of-fact than brusque.

"You were away for training that week," Vince said, returning to my side with only a hint of tension in his posture. His eyes still seemed wary, as if he were braced for an unpleasant surprise. "Colorado, remember?"

"That's right..." Cecil's eyes formed deep creases at the corners. "Frozen armpit of America in the winter—but not too bad in the summer. I stayed a little longer so I could try out some fly fishin'." His eyes lit up with interest. "You fish at all, Angie?"

"Yes, sir," I answered, smiling with genuine enthusiasm. "They don't call Minnesota the land of ten thousand lakes for nothing."

The bill of Cecil's cap lifted in sync with his brow. "Never been there myself. What's good eatin' up there?"

"Mostly sunfish and crappie—they're good pan-fried," I said, with a nonchalant shrug. "But the Pike and Muskie are my favorite, especially beer-battered."

Something about my reply sparked an amiable interest in the man, melting off the aloofness I'd thought I perceived. Cecil went on to ask about ice fishing, and I shared some of my limited experience with frozen lake driving, ice-augers, and the little-known art of using moth grubs as bait. Along the way my uncertainty about the man settled, and so did my stomach.

Vince, meanwhile, tracked our discussion back and forth like a spectator at an invisible ping-pong tournament. "Hey, uh, Dad?" He broke in, after waiting for his father to finish explaining the nuances of a Southern tradition they referred to as "Jugging for Catfish." "You said you wanted to talk to us about something?" Either the anticipation was slaying him slowly, or he just couldn't take any more fish talk. Possibly both.

"Do what, now?" Cecil turned from me and squinted at his son. "Oh, yeah...about that." Clearing his throat he reached out, laying a hand on each of our shoulders. He looked from Vince to me and back with sudden somberness. Then he broke into a broad grin and slapped Vince's shoulder, his chuckle like the low revving of a boat engine. "I was just messin' with you, son."

Cecil gave me a sidelong wink. "I like to keep him on his toes." He released us both and turned, sauntering for the side door. "I'm headin' to meet yer mother down at the bar. Ya'll come on and join us when you get hungry." He threw a wave over his shoulder and was gone.

I looked back to find Vincent's jaw slack, bewilderment fading from his expression. "And...that was my dad. The sadist."

"I think he likes me." I beamed at Vince in satisfaction, nudging his shoulder with mine. "Does he like giving everybody a hard time, or just you?"

"Depends on his mood," Vince shrugged, a trace of humor returning to his voice. "He gets scary creative when he's bored, though."

"How creative?"

"You know that freaky dream I had about the clown—the one I turned into a mini radio play?"

I nodded.

"After he found out about that, and my little aversion to clowns, Dad went and found *that* somewhere in my mom's collection..." Vince motioned across the living room to a glassed-in display case where a small porcelain clown doll sat, its painted-on grin aimed in our direction.

"Oh, dear."

"It gets worse," Vince said, eyeing the doll with excessive wariness. "I woke up one night when it was storming, and my bedroom door was standing wide open. That...thing...was sitting in the doorway holding a kitchen knife." He gave a full-body shudder.

I gaped at him. "Okay, that's just evil." *And brilliant, in a perverse sort of way.*

I smoothed a comforting hand over the back of Vince's taut shoulders, pressing my lips together to hide my amusement. "I guess this explains where you got the inspiration for some of those villains you like to come up with." I kissed his cheek, trying to distract from the ongoing stare-down he was having with the clown figurine. "I think you might need to get yourself a new creative muse."

Vince turned his attention, along with the rest of himself, toward me. "I think I already did." His hands slid around my waist and tugged me to him.

I tucked myself against him and accepted the kiss he so tenderly delivered. His apprehension was gone along with my own. In that moment, I could put off my worry over how fast these two weeks with him would pass. I could forget how difficult it would be to leave my heart on the opposite side of the country.

"Hey," Vince said, drawing his face back and taking my hand. "Is it okay if I give you your Christmas present now? You know I suck at waiting." His face read as some combination of eager and sheepish.

I smirked, curiosity piqued. "Sure."

He shot the porcelain clown one last leery look, backing out of the living room several dramatized steps before leading me into his room.

Everything was the same as I remembered it. Vince's dated wood-panel walls were still accented with fantastical dragon-themed posters, a red-painted bunk bed resting against the far wall. His Miniature Pinscher, Bud, lay sprawled across the lower futon. The thick-bodied dog yawned and stretched at the sight of us, but didn't bother getting up.

It took me a moment to realize I'd expected something to have changed; which was silly, of course. Just because I'd recently put to rest the decorating sense of my 13-year-old self didn't mean Vince felt the same need. As much as we talked about it, he might not be ready to move into a new phase of life just yet.

While Vince rummaged through his closet, I scanned his room and lingered in the memory of my initial visit. These last five months had passed like a surreal lifetime. Still, I could recall our first few days together with all the luminosity of Christmas lights against snow.

My gaze jerked to a halt at the top of his dresser, where a certain picture frame still laid face-down.

The prom photo.

The elegant image of Vince and his two-timing ex-girlfriend appeared as fresh in my mind as the first time I'd seen it. My gut clenched, quaking in the aftermath of a phantom sucker-punch. Why had he kept the picture? If I'd been betrayed and emotionally eviscerated the way Vince had, my first act of coping would have involved a bonfire and all physical reminders of the offender. I'd very nearly done that to everything that could possibly remind me of Scott, and we hadn't even been in an "official" relationship.

Was it possible...had Vince not completely moved on?

"Here it is." Vince sounded triumphant as he backed out of his hanging clothes. "Had to make sure Bud couldn't get a hold of it." He offered out a rectangular box, about the size of a movie case but three times as thick.

I accepted it, forcing a smile to cover the sudden surge of doubt. "If we're doing presents now, you can have yours." I moved to my suitcase and pulled out a silver-wrapped package that actually did contain a movie.

We opened them together. I slid the innards out of my box and carefully examined the foam-wrapped painting. It was a Native-American inspired piece—the image a timber wolf set on a canvas of animal skin and framed by faux stone. "It's beautiful," I said, tracing my finger along the textured frame.

Vince was busy reading the blurb on the back of the movie case. "Is this...that post-apocalyptic dragon movie we almost watched while you were here this summer?"

I nodded, glad he'd remembered. "I think you'll like it."

Wolves and dragons. At least we knew each other's tastes. Even if part of me was afraid it might be past time to set aside some of our adolescent interests.

"Are you....disappointed?" Vince asked, concern pinching at his freckled brow.

"No, no," I answered, a little too quickly. "I love it."

He shifted closer and reached out, setting his fingertips on my elbows. "What's wrong?"

I shook my head and smiled. "Nothing."

"The infamous 'nothing,'" he intoned in a mock-solemn voice. A half-smile tugged at one side of his mouth as he studied me intently. "Your eyes are hazel—almost green. Just tell me what you're thinking about."

So, he hadn't forgotten that my otherwise brown eyes had the odd tendency to lighten in color the more upset I became. I could hardly complain about his perceptiveness.

I clutched the wolf painting close to my midsection and dropped my gaze for a few long breaths. When I collected myself enough, I looked back up to make sure I caught every minute facet of his face and reaction while I asked, "Is there any particular reason you still have that prom picture of you and your ex?"

Vince's brows shot up, surprise warring with bewilderment for a split second. "Where..." He trailed off as a thought seemed to occur to him. Following my gaze toward the dresser, he dropped his hands back to his sides. "Oh."

"Yeah," I said.

He cupped a palm over the back of his neck in a hangdog look. "To be honest...I totally forgot about that thing." Vince stepped away from me and up to the dresser and then fiddled with the back of the frame until he'd extracted the 8x10 inch picture. Without looking he folded the image in on itself, creasing it once, twice, three times—as if reducing all evidence of his high school romance to nothing more than bad origami. Without another word he leveled a meaningful look at me and then went striding out of his room.

I set down my painting and followed a few steps behind.

Vince walked down the short hall and straight through the lighthouse-themed kitchen. I paused when he stopped in front of a barrel-like garbage can, pulled the lid off, and flung the picture into the bottom. He replaced the lid and turned, looking vaguely surprised to find me watching him. "Now it's where it belongs."

I clasped my opposite wrist with one hand and squeezed, nodding. That was what I wanted to hear—needed to hear. But still, some nagging corner of my brain refused to stop wondering. He'd been alone for a year when I'd met him. Was that enough time to get over so many feelings...so many firsts?

"Come on." Vince freed one of my hands and guided me back through the kitchen, hanging a right into the living room before pulling me down onto the worn blue couch beside him. He reclined back and wrapped me in a strong embrace. I laid my head against his chest, my temple pressed to the curve of his collarbone. His heart thumped a steady rhythm just below my ear. "Don't think about her, okay?" he murmured, pressing a kiss to my brow. "I don't."

"Okay," I said, wishing some thoughts had an off switch. The best I could seem to do was trade one gnawing concern for another. After a few grounding minutes of being held, I said, "You know...at some point while I'm here, we really need to talk about the future. Our future."

I felt Vince tense ever so slightly. If I hadn't been so close, I might not have noticed the unconscious response. "Yeah...I guess we do," he said, his voice betraying hesitancy. "But don't worry about that right now."

"When *should* I worry about it?"

"Let's just enjoy this—get used to being together again for a while." He pet a hand down my arm and slid his fingers between mine.

I closed my eyes and savored the sensation. As much as his blatant avoidance troubled me, I found it hard to argue. "Alright." I took a deep breath and let it out slowly. I lifted my head then, trying out a smile I hoped he'd find persuasive. "I'm used to it."

Vince chuckled, shifting to urge me into a stand. "It's about dinner time—we should head down to the bar. If we wait too late they'll start karaoke, and you'll never think of my mom's voice the same way again."

I took the hint, abandoning my line of questioning as I let him up. I could wait for Vince to want to talk out the details. I just wasn't sure how to wait without reading into his hesitation in the meantime...

~ ~ ~ ~ ~ ~ ~

The next morning Vince was acting strangely.

When I woke up on that Saturday, it took me several minutes to find him pacing out on his parents' back porch. He was on his phone—freshly showered, hair gelled into spikes, and having what seemed like an intense discussion with someone. I opened the door and stepped out into the near-chilly air. Vince's head snapped up and he waved, waiting just a few seconds before cutting off whoever he was talking to with, "Hey, I'll call you back."

"Sorry, I didn't mean to interrupt."

"You didn't," Vince gave me a winsome smile and stepped up to kiss my cheek.

I leaned into him automatically, though my mind was wandering. "Who were you talking to?"

"Just Grady." Vince shrugged, but didn't attempt to elaborate.

"Everything okay?"

"Sure," he said, voice almost cheerfully dismissive. "You know Grady...he likes to talk."

"More than most girls I know." I smirked, still suspicious that Vince and his best friend were keeping something from me. And considering the last few bits of relationship advice he'd gotten from Grady had resulted in varying shades of well-intentioned disaster, I felt justified in being concerned.

Before I could decide how to address his evasiveness, Vince changed the subject.

"We should go for a walk," he said. "It's nice out, and the weather is supposed to get colder after today."

Now I knew something was amiss. True to the computer geek stereotype, Vince had the same fondness for outdoor activities that most cats had for water.

"Sounds nice," I said, not about to discourage his newfound enthusiasm. "Should I get Bud's leash?"

"Nah." He waved off the idea. "You can exercise him later. I'm driving you somewhere."

"Oh," I said, glancing down at my plain everyday clothes—jeans and a camouflage-patterned T-shirt emblazoned with the words, "Ha! Now you can't see me." "Should I change?"

"Why? You look fine," Vince said, moving to the back storm door and holding it open for me. "We're just going to a park."

*A park.* Nothing super secret or suspicious sounding. I took his invitation to head for the car, setting aside any more speculation.

Maybe I was just being paranoid.

Vince was quiet as he drove us ten minutes north. I tried to make conversation, but he seemed distracted. The analytical side of me kicked into high gear and I eventually arrived at two very different explanations: either he was thinking about breaking up with me and just didn't want to do it early in my visit...or he was about to propose.

I was *reasonably* sure the second option was more likely, but the realist in me liked to be prepared for anything.

The little park Vince selected was set back on the nicer side of town. It was scenic enough, with a man-made pond encircled by a gravel walking trail and lined with weeping willows. The realist in me also noticed it was also an open public place, where anyone would be less tempted to make a scene.

Vince parked in the middle of a nearly deserted lot and got out, rounding the front of his car to open my door. I let him. I might never get used to deferring my self-sufficiency in the name of his ingrained sense of courtesy. But I had to admit, I was starting to enjoy it.

He brushed the back of my knuckles with his as I got out and stood, which I interpreted as his way of asking for my hand without being so presumptive as to take it. Either he wasn't especially interested in holding hands, or he was nervous. His expression said he was preoccupied with scanning the park.

The sun was halfway up, gleaming off the calm pond straight ahead. An old man walking a golden retriever was just disappearing into the trees to the left, and a middle-aged woman jogged along the far side of the water. Aside from them, the only other movement was a flock of chubby white ducks gathered along the shoreline.

I reached out and linked my fingers loosely with Vince's, waiting for him to lead the way. But instead of aiming for the walking path he headed straight for a wooden dock that jutted over the pond. At the same time, the mass of ducks came surging up from the shore toward us.

"Should have brought some old bread," Vince said, veering aside with me in tow. "Sorry, guys—nothing edible here."

The ducks were faster than they looked. With a demanding chorus of '*quacks*' the eager fowl swarmed around our legs, nibbling and tugging at our pants as we waded through them. We finally broke through and sprinted for the dock, both of us yelping in total abandonment of dignity. The ducks pursued at first, then slowed.

When my feet hit the wood planks, I started laughing at the absurdity of our getaway. The bemused look on Vince's face cut me short. I glanced back and realized that the ducks hadn't given up...they'd simply yielded to a pack of squirrels. Half a dozen of the gray, bushy-tailed creatures came dashing along the shoreline headed right for us.

I bent to beckon them closer. "How cute!"

"You don't want to do that," Vince warned, urgently clasping my shoulder. "I'm pretty sure there was just an article in the paper about the city having problems with rabid squirrels."

"Oh..." I straightened, suddenly seeing the adorable creatures as disease-addled and sinister. I had a rough idea of how much I didn't want to spend my second visit to Alabama keeping up with three to four rounds of rabies shots. "Do you think they know we've eaten their kinfolk?" I whispered, clinging to humor.

Vince backed us up a few steps. "Whoa—"

I had assumed we were safe standing over open water. I was wrong.

While most of the squirrels stopped at the foot of the dock, two of the more brazen animals bounded on after us. I backpedaled along with Vince until we reached the end of the pier where it formed a 'T'. If there hadn't been railing, I might have jumped off.

They had us cornered.

"Shoo!" I stomped my foot, causing one of the squirrels to hesitate. The other seemed to take it as an invitation. It darted straight for my extended foot, as if intending to climb me. I flattened by back to the railing, certain I was about to end up either bitten or wet. Possibly both.

Vince sprang into action, jumping in front of me and yelling in a comically hostile tone. The nearest squirrel leapt backward and he charged it, waving his arms while shouting incoherently. The two rodents startled into u-turns. Their claws made frantic scrabbling sounds as he chased them back down the length of the dock and onto shore.

I applauded as Vince came striding back, hair glinting copper in the sun and shoulders thrown back in an exaggerated show of victory. Anxiety all but forgotten, I had to laugh. "My hero."

Vince stopped in front of me wearing a proud, boyish grin. He shook his head in a look of amused disbelief. "Well I had this great speech all planned out in my head, but now I can't remember it. So I'll just get to the point before something else happens—" He produced a burgundy-colored velvet box from one of the many pockets of his cargo pants and dropped to one knee as he opened it. "Marry me?"

I gaped down at him.

Thanks to the unexpected assault by local wildlife, I'd all but forgotten my earlier suspicions. I was only aware enough of the ring to reach out and pluck it up—too riveted on the hopefulness in Vince's eyes to focus on anything else. I slid the token onto my left ring finger absently. A light, giddy sensation started in my stomach and drifted upward until I couldn't help but beam from the inside out. "Okay."

*Okay? That didn't sound right...* Was I supposed to start crying and scream, "Yes!"?

Vince got back to his feet and I threw my arms around his shoulders, muffling my laughter as I hugged him until he coughed.

I'd never been one to fantasize about things like weddings or proposals. Even if I had, I couldn't have imagined things going this way. Yet, the whole thing suited me—suited us—just fine. Simple. Sincere. And weirdly wonderful.

I already knew our "ever after" wouldn't always be happy or even comfortable—and clearly it couldn't be expected to go according to plan. Still, it was *ours*. And I felt sure we were both determined enough to see it through to "the end."

"So, I take it the animals weren't in on this," I said, finally drawing back to look at him.

Vince chuckled, and then cast a mock-wary glance over his shoulder. "Apparently I forgot to pay off the duck mafia, or something."

"We can't do anything normal, can we?"

He grinned, causing the skin at the corners of his eyes to crinkle. "I hope not."

I groomed my fingers through the short hair at the nape of his neck, still smiling with uninhibited joy. My cheeks were already beginning to ache, the muscles unused to so much use. "You know...I'd still like to hear that proposal speech one day. Whenever you happen to remember it."

"I might have to save it for some time when you're mad at me," Vince said, a half-smile playing across his face. His expression sobered somewhat, though the serene air of satisfaction remained fixed. "You didn't look at the ring." He stated it as a point of curiosity.

I shrugged. "You could have proposed to me with a soda cap ring—I still would have said yes. I made my mind up about you a long time ago."

Vince's gaze shifted from tender to fervent. I knew that look. My insides quivered, anticipating an imminent kiss. But instead he trailed his fingers along my left arm where it draped over his shoulder. When he found my hand he drew it down, holding it between us. Since he seemed to be studying the ring, I gave it my full attention.

The thin, silvery piece was set with three stones—a brilliant, round diamond flanked by two smaller teardrop sapphires. The lesser stones were so rough cut and blue they were almost black. I flexed my fingers and tried not to think about how many of his meager paychecks the ring likely signified. "It's beautiful," I said, meaning it.

"I designed it." Vince's gaze flickered up and met mine, intently. "Took me a while to find somebody who could make it for me, but it was worth it."

My throat tightened, my body overwhelmed with a sense of fullness I wasn't sure how to contain or respond to. When I didn't say anything, Vince went on.

"The diamond represents God." He ran the pads of his thumbs over my knuckles and around the ring. "The semi-precious stones represent us. You, me, and God in the middle. That's what I want you to remember when you look at it."

He'd just imbued the ring with more value than any jeweler could measure.

Tears pricked behind my eyes, threatening to spill over the emotions I couldn't restrain anymore. But instead of crying I gave them a different outlet, lunging into Vince. I poured my all into a kiss so ardent, a tiny part of me was afraid of injuring one of us.

Vince absorbed my forcefulness without complaint, arms locking around me as he returned every ounce of intensity. We kissed long and deep, with abandon and promise.

By the time we let up, I had to grab the dock railing to steady myself. I pressed my face into the curve of his neck and caught my breath. "Can we just go ahead and get married, already?" I asked in a plaintive tone, only half-joking.

Vince traced his fingers up and down my back, his jaw nuzzling my temple. "The courthouse is just a couple of miles away."

I lifted my head, bringing his face into focus. His eyes shone green and gold in the sunlight, set with a seriousness I couldn't ignore. "You mean...elope?"

He nodded, a faint smile forming on his lips. "No muss, no fuss. No people implying we're too young and dumb to make a decision that's supposed to last a lifetime."

I considered the option at length. I didn't think our parents would actually mind. My parents trusted my judgment—or so they claimed. And Vince's parents had eloped just a few weeks after they'd met.

"You know if we elope, people are going to assume I'm pregnant..."

Vince shrugged and smirked. "Since when do we care about *people* and their assumptions?"

"Good point." I bit back a laugh, absently holding my palm over his heart as I weighed the pros and cons. "It's really tempting."

"But," Vince said, grazing the backs of his fingers against my cheek. "You'd miss out on the pictures, and the dress, and the cake...all the traditional stuff. I don't want you to regret not having any of those memories."

"You just *had* to be reasonable." I leaned into his touch and groaned. I didn't care even half a bit about all the pomp and food and gawking people...but there was one thing my mind dwelled on. "Pictures," I said at last. "All I would really want out of it are some nice pictures we can show our kids someday."

"Then that's what we'll have." Vince lifted my left hand and kissed it, his expression still smoldering with anticipation. "We've waited this long, we can wait a little longer."

I was positive I'd never felt more impatient in my entire life than I did in that moment.

"How about we take that walk you promised," I suggested. *Before I change my mind about the courthouse.*

A slow smile spread across his face, as though he knew exactly what I was thinking. He tucked my hand in the crook of his arm. "Brave the squirrels again, or wait for a distraction?" With a nod to one side of the pond, he indicated the jogger who would be passing in front of the parking lot within the next couple of minutes.

"Distraction," I said.

We strolled back down the dock, unhurried. Vince eyed the roaming gaggle of ducks with exaggerated vigilance. While we paused near the shoreline, I held up my left hand and gave the engagement ring more study. In turning my hand side to side I noticed the stones weren't as symmetrical as I'd first thought. "Did you know the sapphires are different?"

"What?" Vince shifted his attention my way to peer at the ring.

I held my hand out to him and bent my fingers to show him the side view. "See? One of them is almost twice as thick as the other one."

"Huh. You're right. I hadn't noticed." His brow creased for a thoughtful moment. He shrugged then, forming a satisfied half-smile. "I guess that makes it all the more unique. Just like us."

Amusement tickled at the back of my mind. "So, if the sapphires are supposed to represent you and me...I guess I must be the thicker one."

"Whoa...hey..." Vince sputtered. "That's a trap." He took a step back and threw up his hands in the universal signal of surrender. "You couldn't pay me to walk into that little funhouse of doom."

"I'm kidding!" I followed his retreat and hugged his side, laughing. "Sorry. Couldn't resist."

Vince gradually relaxed under my hold. His arm dropped to encircle my shoulders, keeping me tucked to his side as we waited for a break in our standoff with Mother Nature.

"I'll have to get you a wedding band—make sure it's obvious you're off the market," I mused aloud.

"Middle-school girls everywhere will be so disappointed." He smirked aside at me, making light of the fact that his youthful appearance tended to attract unwanted attention from thirteen and fourteen-year-olds.

I chuckled, leaning into him. "Any preferences in rings?"

"Nah." He shook his head. "Just one request, if you decide to get it engraved."

I straightened up to look at him, curious. "Sure. What do you want it to say?"

Vince lifted his chin, cutting a dramatic profile as he let a pause drag out. He raised his free arm then and made a sweeping motion as he quoted from *Lord of the Rings* in a resounding voice, "One ring to rule them all!"

"*Very* romantic," I said, dissolving into laughter. When I caught my breath I also caught Vince grinning at me, wearing the familiar look of triumph he always had after making me smile.

Oh, yes. This was going to be an interesting life.

# Postface

Dear Reader,

Thank you for allowing me to share this part of my life's story. If you've also read *Once Upon a Road Trip*, I am doubly grateful you chose to pick up this continuation.

For the sake of closure, you should know that Vincent and I did indeed get married that following July, in Minnesota — a year to the day we met for the first time in "real life." Grady stood as Best Man and Elsie as Maid of Honor. (And amazingly, no undue vandalism or injuries resulted.) I wore a borrowed dress, my sister sang, and Vince and I began our union by soundly assailing each other with strawberry cake. It was magnificent.

We drove down to Alabama the day after the wedding, and here we've stayed. At the publication of this book we have been married for 11 years. In that time we've had a theme park's share of ups and downs, but I wouldn't trade this life for all the sweet tea in the South. It has been my great privilege to finish growing up with my best friend.

These days we're kept busy rearing a son and daughter — who are, in my shamelessly biased opinion, turning out to be brilliant little human beings. Vince and I still enjoy video games, but generally prefer the ones that allow us to 'pause' for reality.

Thanks to the advancement of various forms of social media, I've been able to either maintain or reestablish contact with a number of my original online friends. I still hope to try out a West Coast road trip one day. (In an effort to be pragmatic, I'm holding out for a midlife crisis.) But this time around, it won't be a solo venture.

Who knows? I might even let Vince drive.

~Ang

# Acknowledgements

First and foremost, thank you to God — the ultimate Author and illustrator of my life's story. 1 Corinthians 13:4-7

Thank you to Courtney Wichtendahl, for your undying generosity and the insightful ways you've affected both me and my writing. I treasure your friendship.

Thanks also to my RWA sisters (the Heart of Dixie, Music City, and Southern Magic chapters) for all the years of encouragement, critiquing, and camaraderie.

Special thanks to M.V. Freeman, Katherine Bone, and C.J. Redwine for all of the personal and professional cheerleading...and otherwise putting up with my anguished whining.

A huge thank you to my faithful sisters-in-spirit, Katherine "Kitten" DeVoe and Patience Holloway.

To Ian Cavanaugh, Michelle Gullixson, Bonny Buchanan, and Andrea Robinson, for your fearless literary input and loyal support.

Many boatloads of pre-screened gratitude to my teen beta readers: Jon-Michael, Lana, Tatya, Kelly, and Anna.

Thank you to Danielle of *Inspire by Danielle* for her stellar photography work, and to Mollie Fischer, my lovely-yet-ambiguous cover model.

Thanks always to my parents for supporting and wanting the best for me, regardless.

To Robin Roberts for being my "extra mommy," even all these years after I first showed up on your doorstep with a roadmap and crazy dream.

And last but never least, thank you to my readers—both the new and the ones who first read *Once Upon a Road Trip* and asked to hear more of the story. Without your open curiosity and support, this anthology wouldn't exist.

# Book Club Discussion Questions

1. How would you describe your experience with this book? Were you engaged immediately, or did it take you a while to "get into it?"

2. Describe the main character, Angeli — personality, motivations, self-perception.

3. What main ideas/themes does the author explore in this anthology?

4. Were any events in this book relevant to your own life in some way?

5. Did a specific passage, quote, or scene elicit a strong reaction from you — good or bad? Share the passage and its effect.

6. If you could ask the author a question, what would you ask?

7. Have you read other books by this author? If so, how does this book compare? If not, does this book inspire you to read others?

8. Has this story broadened your perspective in any way? Have you learned something new, or been exposed to a different way of looking at something?

9. Compare this anthology to other memoirs you may have read. Is it similar to any of them?

10. What do you think will be your lasting impression of this book?

# About The Author

Angela N. Blount is a Minnesota native, transplanted to the deep South--where she currently resides with her understanding husband, their two children, and a set of identity-confused cats. She is a former book reviewer for RT Book Reviews, a memoirist, freelance editor, sporadic poet, and webcomic artist.

In her spare time, Angela enjoys reading, coffee shop loitering, questionable attempts at horticulture, and all things geeky.

Find out more about Angela and her latest projects here:
**http://www.angelanblount.com/**

**Facebook:** https://www.facebook.com/AngelaNBlount

**Twitter:** https://twitter.com/Perilous1

## Also by
# Angela N. Blount

## "...sometimes, in the middle of nowhere, you find yourself."

Eighteen-year-old Angeli doesn't "fit in." She's never been on a single date, and she lives vicariously through an online world of storytelling. With the pressures of choosing a practical future path bearing down, she needs a drastic change. Too old to run away from home, she opts instead to embark on a solo 2-month road trip. But her freedom is tempered by loneliness - and anxiety tests her resolve as she comes face-to-face with her quirky internet friends.

Aside from contracting mono and repeatedly getting

herself lost, Angeli's adventure is mired by more unforeseen glitches - like being detained by Canadian authorities, and a near-death experience at the hands of an overzealous amateur wrestler. Her odyssey is complicated further when she unwittingly earns the affections of two young men. One a privileged martial artist; the other a talented techie with a colorful past.

Bewildered by the emotions they stir, Angeli spurns the idea of a doomed long-distance relationship. But she is unprepared for the determination of her hopeful suitors. In the wake of her refusal, one man will betray her, and the other will prove himself worthy of a place in her future.

Angeli sets off in search of a better understanding of herself, the world, and her place in it. What she finds is an impractical love, with the potential to restore her faith in happy endings.

A true story with an unapologetically honest outlook on life, love, faith, and adventure - *Once Upon A Road Trip* is a coming-of-age memoir.

ARTIFICE
PRESS
™

Made in the USA
Charleston, SC
08 October 2014